PRAISE FOR
LIFE CHAPTERS

"*Life Chapters* is a literary thrust into another world. It is a profound challenge to the materialist assumption that consciousness perishes with physical death. This account is consistent with the emerging evidence that consciousness is infinite in space and time, therefore immortal, eternal, and one."

—**Larry Dossey, MD**
Author of *Healing Words* and *The Power of Premonitions*

"This book speaks volumes on the greatest issues before men and women in relationship today—intimacy, trust, and spiritual connection—and the paths we choose to work out those issues. I applaud Dr. Stoller's bravery and honesty in sharing his journey."

—**Leslie Carol Botha**
Health educator and broadcast journalist

"Expansion…connection…learning…joy. I closed Galen's book and these are the words that lingered, each describing an experience of the afterlife. Featured are stories of people who journeyed through earth and are continuing their evolution on 'the other side.' Amazing how our quirks and personalities carry forward yet our life lessons are wondrously enhanced and reinforced. Uplifting to know that what we can gain 'there' can also be accessed 'here.' How very narrow is the bridge of light between life and death."

—**Cyndi Dale**
Intuitive consultant and author of *The Subtle Body, Energetic Boundaries* and *The Intuition Guidebook*

"This book gives a new understanding to the emotions of grief, fear, love, and connection. It inspires the reader to contemplate how their own beliefs can shape and limit their experience in this life and beyond. Galen's words provide great comfort to me, confirming that the energetic fields I experience with this earthly body are but small glimpses of what exists in the afterlife and further clarifying what I know in my heart to be the true nature of existence."

—**Angela Levesque**
Mind/body educator, energy healer, and radio host

"Dr. Stoller's fearless translation of his son Galen's afterlife experience and soul growth is a vital contribution to those of us who grieve the loss of our loved ones. The information shared by Galen can inspire us to focus on our own soul's contract by seeking to understand the lessons offered by The University of Earth and doing our best to make a positive difference on the planet."

—**Lo Anne Mayer**
Author of *Celestial Conversations*

"Beautifully written and inspiring, *Life Chapters* is a must read for those who seek to understand that there truly is an all-pervasive life force to which we are all connected, that there is 'life after life,' and that love is forever."

—**Barb Adams**
Host, *Amerika Now* talk radio show

Volume 2 in the Death Walker Series

Life Chapters

extraordinary afterlives of people you never heard of

GALEN STOLLER
(1991–2007)

Edited by K Paul Stoller, MD
Foreword by Fiona Bowie, PhD

Dream Treader Press
Santa Fe and San Francisco

Published by: Dream Treader Press
　　　　　　　404 Brunn School Road #E
　　　　　　　Santa Fe, NM 87505
　　　　　　　www.dreamtreaderpress.com

Copyeditors: Ellen Kleiner and Terri Daniel
Book design and production: Janice St. Marie

Copyright © 2012 by K Paul Stoller

All rights reserved. No portion of this book, except for brief reviews, may be reproduced, stored in retrieval systems, or transmitted in any form or by any means—electronic, mechanical, photocopying, recording, or otherwise—without written permission of the publisher.

A portion of the proceeds from the sale of this book will be donated to organizations around the world dedicated to the sustainability of assistance and search & rescue dogs.

First edition

Printed in the United States of America

Publisher's Cataloging-in-Publication Data

Stoller, Galen, 1991-2007 (Spirit)
　　　Life chapters : extraordinary afterlives of people you never heard of / Galen Stoller ; edited by K Paul Stoller. -- Santa Fe, N.M. : Dream Treader Press, c2012.

　　　　　p. ; cm.
　　　(Death walker series ; vol. 2)

　　　ISBN: 978-0-9832425-2-9

　　　　　1. Stoller, Galen, 1991-2007. 2. Future life. 3. Spiritualism. 4. Parapsychology. 5. Children--Death--Psychological aspects. 6. Spiritualists--Biography. 7. Guides (Spiritualism). I. Stoller, K Paul. II. Title III. Series: Stoller, Galen, 1991-2007 (Spirit).
　　　　　Death walker series ; v. 2.

BF1311.F8 G352 2012　　　　　　　　　　2011934531
133.901/3--dc22　　　　　　　　　　　　2012

1　3　5　7　9　10　8　6　4　2

To those who ask why
and to those who know
that there is something beyond
the life they are living,
that there is a reason for being

CONTENTS

Foreword by Fiona Bowie, PhD   9
Prologue   15
CHAPTER ONE: First Breath   23
CHAPTER TWO: Charles Miller   33
CHAPTER THREE: Monica   43
CHAPTER FOUR: Benjamin   57
CHAPTER FIVE: Arthur and Eileen   65
CHAPTER SIX: Sally   73
CHAPTER SEVEN: Mr. Montpelier   81
CHAPTER EIGHT: The Tsunami Family   91
CHAPTER NINE: The Travelers   101
CHAPTER TEN: Daniel   111
CHAPTER ELEVEN: Barbara   119
CHAPTER TWELVE: Beth   127
CHAPTER THIRTEEN: Jaloo   137
CHAPTER FOURTEEN: All Dogs Go to Heaven (Sort of)   149
CHAPTER FIFTEEN: Nathaniel   159
CHAPTER SIXTEEN: Angels   167
Epilogue   173

Foreword

To some, the stories in this book will no doubt seem fanciful, the result of an active imagination—essentially fiction. This is not, however, how the book's author and editor see them. For starters, the author, Galen Stoller, can speak with unusual authority as he died in 2007 in an accident, as a young man of sixteen. The editor, K Paul Stoller, is his father, who sought to overcome his grief and reestablish connection with his son via a talented medium. Their communications were not limited to an occasional dream or coincidence, but resulted in a flood of detailed information on what was happening to Galen in his new life, initially described in *My Life after Life*, published in 2011. This second book continues where the first left off, but focuses less on Galen and more on other inhabitants of the afterlife dimension he presently inhabits. These sixteen stories are regarded as true accounts, in as much as the limits of human understanding and the translation from one dimension to another can apprehend them. Most concern people who have lived human lives in the fairly recent past, while some have experienced nonhuman existence, and often accompanying the humans are animals and angels.

These life stories are rendered with a sense of purpose and urgency as father and son, separated but still joined through the barrier of death, explore life and its consequences from both sides. How one lives and how one dies are, we are told, important in determining the nature of postmortem existence. In each story, what people bring with them to the afterlife, especially their beliefs and personality traits, affect where they go and what happens to them. If someone dies believing they will be transported straight to heaven, with angels in white playing harps, this is likely to be their first experience—not because this is what heaven is like but because those who meet the newly arrived will take on the form or forms that best enable them to make the transition to this new dimension. Beliefs, the thoughts we accept as true, create "reality," albeit one that passes in due course. Theosophy, a spiritual philosophy originating in the late nineteenth century, has long taught that thought has a physical component and real consequences. We may not see these clearly on earth, but in the afterlife dimensions thought is the chief vehicle of creation. The houses, fields, rivers, halls of learning, and all the other features of Galen's world are the product of human (and nonhuman) thought created and given solidity by those who inhabit that plane.

For example, just after he arrived in the afterlife Galen was met by a search and rescue dog named Andy, who, as portrayed in *My Life after Life*, was able to provide him with a sense of connection and comfort. Andy turned out to be a highly intelligent being who had chosen the form of a dog Galen had been particularly close to on earth. In another instance, described in *Life Chapters*, a deceased person's guide took the form of family members he had expected would greet him when he passed over. Although family members often do greet new arrivals, expectations also help inform the reception an individual will experience. This is perhaps clearest and most dramatic in the case of those who expect nothing, who are unprepared to step out of one body and into another. In such cases, the initial period of readjustment might be longer and harder, although helped by the prayers and love of those left behind and the patience of the guides waiting to receive them.

The descriptions of Galen's adventures can be seen as part of a genre of postmortem accounts that dates back centuries. The Greek poet Pindar, who died around 440 BC, is said to have dictated some poems in honor of Persephone through one of his female relatives a few days after he died. In his *Dialogues*, the sixth-century pope Gregory the Great gives several accounts of the afterlife from those who had undergone near-death experiences (had died but been sent back and returned to consciousness). Their stories, familiar from more recent literature, tell of the pleasant meadows and houses bathed in a bright white light that await the righteous, and the gloomy depressing regions to which those who delighted in cruelty are drawn (or sent). More recently, British army officer T.E. Lawrence, desperate to leave behind the infamy that had earned him the epithet Lawrence of Arabia, revealed through the Quaker medium Jane Sherwood that he had died quite unprepared, with no belief in the continued existence of the soul. He had consequently found himself wandering in a gray loveless region inhabited by those who had done little to advance themselves humanly or spiritually. After a short while, he was "rescued" and transported to a dimension in which he could find peace and work to rid himself of ingrained habits of mind, the pride and the prejudices that had no currency in his current realm of existence.

In a sense, *Life Chapters* can also be seen as a collection of morality tales, the postmortem equivalent of medieval mystery plays. Each of the stories carries a lesson the reader can reflect upon and learn from, returning to those most moving and powerful at various times and in different moods. Whether they are taken at face value or as fiction does not ultimately matter, as the lessons will in any case reach those who are receptive to them. When another of Jane Sherwood's discarnate interlocutors described the problems of transmitting knowledge from other planes through the limitations of an incarnate human mind, he discovered that successful mediums often had a deep, unconscious intimation of something recognized and loved. Readers of *Life Chapters* may catch that fleeting sense of the familiar, like the coattails of a well-known friend disappearing from sight. After all, we are told that our periods on earth are brief interludes in a much longer and more vivid life spent in dimensions similar to Galen's. We travel there in our dreams and may awaken with a sense of nostalgia. Thus, despite the lack of conclusive scientific evidence capable of convincing children of our post-Enlightenment materialist world of the reality of such realms, Galen's stories are not as fanciful as some people might imagine.

Readers are invited to take these tales at face value and to use the intuitive faculties we have all been granted to assess their worth and veracity. In this light, the tales both confirm and add to many similar accounts passed on through mediums, from those who have undergone near-death experiences, who have gained glimpses of interlife states by means of hypnotic regression, or who have explored these dimensions in an altered state of consciousness. Together they paint a picture of a world that is at once fascinating, challenging, and satisfying—certainly nothing like the rather tedious image of sitting around on clouds watching angels play their harps. As these life chapters attest, those whose greatest fear of heaven is eternal boredom need have no further worry.

—Fiona Bowie, PhD
Honorary Research Fellow in Archaeology
and Anthropology
University of Bristol, UK

Although drawn by my great-aunt for my father when he turned twenty-one, given the imagery this sketch could have been prophetically about me.

Prologue

In this dimension on the "other side," I have gained a great deal more experience since providing my father with the content of our first book, *My Life after Life: A Posthumous Memoir*. I now match the maturity of my father as a teacher, even though by earth cycles I am just turning twenty-one years old. In *Life Chapters,* I describe the life paths of several individuals I have encountered here to provide additional information about this dimension.

Since coming to the other side, I have been increasingly interested in observing the arrival of others and noticing how aspects they bring with them, especially their personality traits and beliefs, impact their entry and integration into this dimension. For instance, new arrivals, usually from earth, are often accompanied by teachers whose appearance seems influenced by the path their arrival is walking. In other words, a teacher's appearance reflects what the student expects to be focusing on in this dimension. My teacher looks like a middle-aged scholarly man with a graying beard, representing my potential for becoming a teacher while in this dimension. The teacher of a more recent arrival was like a mother helping her child off the school bus to take her home. Another teacher assembled several family members the new graduate believed would be here on his arrival.

I have watched a parade of individuals of various ages, backgrounds, and energies entering this dimension and leaving through a different quadrant. It is evident when individuals come or go: you can sense a change in the energy field surrounding them. While leaving, they are shown the deepest respect. Those who are soon to return to earth emit a blue glow, reflecting an alteration in their chemistry as they prepare to reintegrate with matter. The edges of new arrivals, on the other hand, are usually a little blurry and undefined because their energy fields haven't completely coalesced. The more sudden and unprepared they were to leave their physical body, the more undefined their edges will be.

Sometimes the ones with blurry edges will integrate fairly quickly, but other times they will not, as was my experience. Instead, they may be left in their own space to gather energy as they come to understand their experiences, all the while working with their teachers in preparation to integrate. Or multiple teachers may be called in to facilitate their integration. Soon after my arrival, I was joined by a teacher in the form of a dog named Andy, who held a certain energy for me and acted as my constant companion.

The protocol for greeting arrivals is simple. Until the edges of individuals become defined, you don't approach them any more than you would eat a freshly baked cookie straight out of the oven before it has had a chance to cool off. That is, you give them privacy while they are processing. Unlike on earth, where people are often oblivious to what others are dealing with, here discretion is always part of the conversation, especially with arrivals. There is no list of rules and regulations to follow here; you just instinctively know when you can interact with someone. It is like knowing when a class is being offered that you want to attend.

In addition to the pervasive sense of knowingness in this dimensional realm, all interactions have a flow. I noticed this right after I arrived and was trying to learn how things operate here. Soon an incredible flow became such an integral part of me that I experienced myself in a stream of connectedness en route to knowingness. This phenomenon can also be experienced on the earth, but most people there are so involved in the experience of polarity, the operative teaching paradigm of the earth plane, that the opportunity to tap into the flow under the polarity—through either observation or meditation—is often missed. Yet one can always tune in to it if the desire is there. There are many whose favorite dimension is the earth because of its predictably unpredictable nature—predictable by virtue of its polarity, but unpredictable in terms of the many ways to challenge polarity.

I am explaining these things to help correct a misunderstanding about heaven. No one is floating around on clouds admiring their wings or is blissed out with nothing to do. The truth is that the only joy the soul and spirit have is in gaining experience and a deeper sense of oneness. These objectives, too, can be achieved on earth, although it is a little easier here—and in some respects, a little more difficult as well.

For instance, bringing in any of the earth's religious beliefs about death can limit one's experience of the afterlife, which actually is governed by a natural law ensuring that energy is never destroyed but is transformed into states no longer constrained by laws of the old state. Just as water molecules can be in vapor, clouds, rain, snow, or ice, and while behaving differently in each state they are still water molecules, the same holds true for consciousness. It can change its appearance and behavior from one state to another without being destroyed. It can even revert back to a prior state but not convey the same experience as before because opportunities and choices have changed.

The dogma of religion can make it difficult for some arrivals to cultivate the perception that here everything changes because below the stream of life there is an ever expanding universe. Since this is so, the richest experiences are those that utilize as many levels as possible—physical, emotional, mental, and spiritual. The soul is often drawn back to work with such experiences.

When arriving in the afterlife, not everyone lands in the dimensional realm I am in. Rather, individuals typically arrive in the realm that is most compatible with their skills and abilities in order to enhance their growth. This dimensional station is where it had been agreed that I would continue my education. In the first book of this series, I called my dimensional station, which resonates subtly with earth experience, level 21 for purposes of identification, but here it is not actually called level 21. Each level below this one is more controlled, giving its occupants a chance to develop their perceptions and awareness, while each level above is more expansive.

Individuals who were fractured by their experience on earth, such as those who committed suicide, arrive at a level with a more restrictive environment, where the energy is slow and rhythmic, so that they can integrate their broken selves. This modality is akin to being in a full body cast with limbs suspended by ropes and pulleys. I am not judging suicide, but simply explaining that it results in a different type of experience here and recuperation can take a very long time.

Each level here exudes a climate of energy to support a certain vibration. Level 21 supports my vibration, making it easier for me to create. But being at one level rather than another is not elitist. A polar bear is no better than an African elephant because it can survive amidst Arctic ice, and an elephant is not superior to a polar bear because it is better suited to survive on the African savanna. Certain climates of energy are simply more advantageous for particular vibrations. So if an individual's healing is best done in the tropics, that person will not be sent to Siberia.

By contrast, in moving to another level, as Carl, my younger brother in my extended spiritual family, has been doing by constantly visiting me from level 17, a person may actually adapt to the higher vibration and evolve. Energy always finds a way to fulfill a soul agreement that serves the highest good for all, regardless of whether it takes place in one life or the next, in this dimension or another.

✇ ✇ ✇

Editor's note: Those on earth who prioritize their connection to the energy flowing beneath the stream of polarity are often considered mystics. However, mysticism, which is not a religion but a way of life, receives little or no support in Western society. What does receive support is what I call "missed"icism: dogma, or "authorized truths," that encourage us to deny or remain ignorant of the energetic messages around us, thus suppressing our innate drive to know self and spirit. But "missedicism," although seemingly the unofficial religion of Western society, serves no one. Worse, as a result of its widespread influence many Westerners are missing the whole point of being on planet earth, which is to consciously evolve back to the wholeness from which the human experience isolated us. Wholeness, after all, is our natural state.

Humanity has not always been so alienated from its natural state, but in our world of polarity, where fear and ego are fed daily by dogma, entire generations have had their connection to nature "bred" out of them. As a result, much of their perception is governed by loss.

The world's religions all remind us of a stream of interconnectedness but are often caught up in the play of polarity, expressed in dogmas rife with judgment and separation. The plants and the animals we share the planet with, connected as they are to a more unifying stream of consciousness, beckon us to connect with it too and live in balance with nature. By tapping into it, we can learn to hold apparent opposites—light and dark, success and failure, joy and anger—in balance so they coexist without destroying one another or canceling each other out. Living in a polarized world does not have to result in unending war. There can be balance, as nature is always trying to teach us.

Galen's first book, *My Life after Life: A Posthumous Memoir*, provided an understanding of how people need not wait until they are on the other side to obtain realization, or knowledge of how reality works and how inseparable we are from it. In this context, reality is what is real for everyone everywhere, at all times, including every level and layer of our universe, which is but one of many universes. *My Life after Life* also addressed aspects of the other side, providing some clarity for the curious, even though Galen's experiences there are uniquely his own. This second book, *Life Chapters*, focuses more on how affected we are by the personality traits and beliefs we bring with us to the afterlife, all of which can be changed during our time on earth, thus allowing for a smoother entry and integration when it is our turn to cross over to the other side.

CHAPTER 1

First Breath

One day when I was attending a class I was intuitively drawn to, I noticed three women I had not seen before whispering among themselves. The lecture, which focused on some of the finer points about the silver cup each of us is given on arrival in this dimension and how it preserves information about experiences we had on earth, did not make a big impression on me; instead, my attention was to the three women who were chattering and giggling. As I stared at them, to my surprise all three turned to face me with a "what do you think you are looking at" expression on their faces. This was the first time since arriving that I felt anything close to confrontation with others. It was, in a sense, refreshing as it reminded me of some of the looks I used to get from my friends on earth.

After class, I caught up with them, as is my usual manner when I come across interesting individuals. The women looked like they were in their early thirties, even though they kept giggling as if they were young schoolgirls. As I approached them, I introduced myself, but they gave me the brush-off, which I took in stride, saying, "Okay, then, I will catch up with you later." Soon after, I encountered them again and introduced myself, still curious about them. I could tell they were more grounded than when I had first seen them, but was surprised when they acted as if they hadn't seen me before. After insisting they had no recollection of *me*, they introduced themselves as Ellen, Sarah, and Margit.

"You seem to really know each other, as if you were sisters. Did you know each other on earth?" I asked, interested in how they might have been connected with one another.

They said they had arrived at about the same time but were from diverse parts of the world and had had very different experiences, except for one defining similarity—all three had been pregnant when they had passed. Margit had been in her first trimester, Ellen had been six months pregnant, and Sarah very close to giving birth. They were all aware of when they had died, and each had experienced the anguish of knowing her unborn child would die along with her.

They had also been surprised that upon arriving here with their teachers and being briefed about what had happened, they did not look pregnant and there were no other souls accompanying them and no sense of loss. Only later did they remember they had been pregnant and afraid of their children dying with them.

"Have you since found out what occurred?" I asked.

All three shook their heads no and said they hadn't even asked anyone what had happened. Apparently they weren't worried enough to ask about their unborn children, though this had been their greatest concern while transitioning. But all I could think was that if I died while pregnant I would want to know where the baby went.

"When you were in the classroom, you were all sitting together giggling among yourselves and acting younger than you are now," I observed.

Sarah replied, "Sometimes we feel very lighthearted and happy, like children, but at other times we act our age as we are now."

I found these behavior changes interesting, as I had never experienced anything similar, and felt compelled to get some answers. So I went back to the classroom where I had first met the women and asked the teacher, "What happens to the child when a pregnant woman passes?"

The teacher explained: "The child being carried is a complete and separate individual with its own agreement and path. Even though carried in the body of the mother and conceived from the genetic material of her and the father, the spirit, free will, and choice of that child was intact before conception. So if the physical body of the mother is unable to hold the material that has come together, and the child never completely develops in physical form, that soul is released from the experience. Only when children take their first breath is the agreement between the spiritual, mental, emotional, and physical bodies finalized. That is the soul contract."

The teacher further explained that such babies developing in the womb are conscious and could quickly manifest another connection with a different mother if it served their contract. But since none of the children in this case was under contract when they became separate from their mothers, at the moment the mothers' bodies could no longer support them they began their own journeys back to soul experience. As humans, we consider babies throughout nature to be innocent and in need of protection, especially baby mammals, but the teacher assured me that even babies who are not fully developed have the free will and choice to no longer continue living in their host's body and are capable of moving through such experiences without being traumatized.

Then I asked the teacher, "When I first met them, these women were like children themselves, but when I met them again they acted more mature. What is happening to these women?"

"Often when someone arrives during a pregnancy, they work through the parent-child relationship they did not get to experience on earth by being childlike at times. This phenomenon does not happen with everyone who has been pregnant, but some process their grief in this way," he replied.

It appeared that each of these women had been so connected to the survival of her child that she was processing her loss through her physical body.

For me, this was a lesson in the importance of free will and choice in particular circumstances. No one is completely locked into experiences by others. It could be argued that those who are imprisoned and tortured are evidence against such a statement, but everyone still has free will, even if that just means in our imagination.

❧ ❧ ❧

Editor's note: The information Galen provided helped me understand an experience I had as a pediatric resident in training at UCLA. At one point I had a recurring dream in which I saw a newborn in a baby warmer off in the distance under a spotlight. Every time I approached the warmer, a medical problem was presented to me relevant to that newborn. And when had I solved the problem each dream ended.

Early one morning after several such dreams, I was called to the delivery room and saw the anesthesiologist trying to intubate an infant. This was a bad sign, as an anesthesiologist is never to abandon his patient, the mother, to attend to her infant. He was relieved to be handing off the laryngoscope to me, as he had been unable to get air into the lungs of this baby. I placed the endotracheal tube correctly into the trachea, but when I applied pressure to the neonatal Ambu bag, the infant's small chest didn't move. Apparently there had not been enough amniotic fluid to inflate the lungs, so they had never developed. I realized this was the concluding episode of my dream series played out in real life, and ending with the presentation of an unsolvable medical problem.

It had been impossible for this child to take his first breath, and Galen's account, describing the implications of such an event for an infant, enhanced my understanding of it from a more universal perspective. Although the infant had been conscious and intimately connected to the mother's experience, his agreement to be in that life could not be made until his first breath was taken, and so was never finalized. Consciousness starts with conception, but integration begins with the first breath.

As a pediatrician, I also wanted to find out from Galen what happens to those who pass at a very young age, such as a six-month-old girl I had heard about who was killed by a falling tree branch that struck both her and her mother as they posed for a photo in Central Park. Galen explained that those who are under the age of nine months, even though they have started to develop a personality and to interact consciously with the environment, belong less to the earth dimension and more to spirit, a layer that exists between where we leave our physical bodies and where we eventually leave the earth plane. This place is like a vessel that contains the material of which all things are made. Energy forming in infants who pass moves back into this space that is rich with innocence and beauty, and connected to Source.

Combining the information Galen had presented, I could see that sometimes a soul only needs the experience of conception or birth to complete an understanding. Having that piece of experience in their silver cup when they pass allows them to create a very imaginative persona in the next incarnation, with the ability to maintain childlike wonderment and creativity throughout their life, always connected to a creative flow. There are souls who choose to have limited earth experiences for this reason.

Even if breath is drawn only one time and a new personality is initiated, that limited experience goes into the silver cup that holds the personality's perspective. In the case of only one or two breaths, the silver cup would be very small. A child so young would be placed very carefully into the next experience, making sure it continues the previous agreement.

When children die in utero, there is no personality yet, nor enough experience to maintain the silver cup, so their form goes right back to Source, for in a sense it never left; like firecrackers that never went off, all the material is returned from whence it came. Children who die after nine months of age will process their departure by arriving at the next level of experience then quickly recycling the experience of their time here, which their souls will use over the course of their evolution. It is likely that eventually every soul incarnating on earth will have the experience of leaving at a very young age.

While I would like to think this information might comfort grieving parents, in my own case I don't know if I will ever be able to separate myself from the experience of my son's departure. Raising a child involves a deep commitment, and in the animal kingdom the longer that commitment, the longer the period of grief if the child passes. Only the parental commitment of elephants comes close to that of humans. Of course, the level of commitment among humans varies from one to the next, as does the period of grieving, but if circumstances were to follow nature's dictates, such a commitment would last twelve years, by which time most children could fend for themselves, at least in a world harmonious with nature.

Parental attachments endure a long time in our society because nature has instilled within the family an instinct to maintain its integrity. Instinct also helps individuals process grief. When facing the profundity of my grief at Galen's passing, I kept saying to myself that I had to find the ground under my feet, and my instinct kept moving me toward healing.

CHAPTER 2

Charles Miller

Most of the individuals I've been able to engage in heart-to-heart conversations are people I met in classrooms, and that's where I met Charles Miller. Each classroom is familiar and yet different. The basic architecture is always the same, but they take on the characteristics of the teacher, the subject matter, and the students, not unlike earth classrooms decorated by teachers to express the theme being studied.

One day I was drawn into a room where ten individuals were seated in classic classroom seats, with desks connected to the chairs, as seen in many earth classrooms. I sat across the aisle from a gentleman who had squeezed his tall, lanky body into his chair, leaning back uncomfortably to give his legs adequate room. He seemed to be in his mid- to late forties; had strong facial features, including deeply set eyes; and appeared very wise.

Extremely attracted to this man for some reason, I greeted him by nodding, and he returned my nod. When class was over and he headed out of the building, I followed him and introduced myself.

He said his name was Charles Miller, in what seemed like a dialect from the east coast of the United States. I then asked, "Do you know exactly how long you have been here?"

I realized that no one here actually knows how much time has passed since they left the earth plane. We simply do not experience linear time here. No one celebrates birthdays, and there are no calendars or holidays, so there is no way to gauge how much earth time has passed since our arrival. But I wanted to get a sense of how long the man thought he had been here. I also asked because the man didn't look modern.

Charles rubbed his forehead and said, "I think I have been here quite a while. I was born in 1841, and I died in 1863. But beyond that I have no idea how long I have been here. I do know I am coming to a time when I want to have an experience different from the one I am having now." Taking into consideration the dates of his life and the dates of my own, I calculated that Charles has been here around 150 earth years, and yet there were still things he held on to from his last incarnation, such as his mannerisms and dialect. The cup hanging around his neck was much larger than mine, so I knew he had had many experiences that had given him great wisdom and insight.

"What did you do on earth?" I asked.

"I was a sailor on a ship named *The Madeleine*. My father was a sailor, so being a sailor was the most obvious career for me. I had a wife and a child whom I didn't see often because I was sailing so much. Then one day during a storm I was swept out to sea and drowned."

As he continued his explanation, it became clear that his whole life had been dedicated to activities on his ship, which had, in essence, replaced his wife and child as his main focus. In some ways, he now regretted that he had let something like his ship "steal" his life from him. He wondered what would have happened if he had made different choices. But when he recounted what it had been like to constantly experience the rhythmic motion of the ocean and rely on his instincts and abilities, it became clear that being at sea had given him insight and wisdom, which was reflected in his glowing face.

At times, the motion of the waves would cause him to experience shifts in consciousness and he could see beautiful beings whom he called angels walking across the water. He drew them in his journal and had images of some of them tattooed on his body. His life was the ship, the ocean and its creatures, the dome of the sky, the angels, and his thoughts.

Eventually, during a storm Charles Miller was swept out to sea by a large wave while he was on deck among the gaps between the rigging stays. He floated until he became so cold and disoriented that he sank beneath the rough waves. Just before that, however, he had seen lights sparkling through the water and thought perhaps the storm had broken. But it was too late for him, as he had no strength left to swim to the surface.

His first memory of this dimension was of being lifted up by two very strong men who deposited him on a dry beach. Even though he was dripping with seawater and too tired to stand, as he looked into the faces of his rescuers he experienced greater love and compassion than he had ever before encountered, and he began to weep in the presence of these beings he called angels.

The angels handed him his silver cup and asked him what he would like to know. He inquired about the regrets he had in his life as a result of his choices and how he could truly heal. Then he started to panic, realizing that his wife and child would not know what had happened to him until a message got back to them. He found comfort when his rescuers explained the purpose of his life plan and told him his family would be all right, that according to other agreements his wife would remarry and they all would thrive.

As he was relating this, I could see the pain in his eyes, and I assumed this was the reason he was still here, his regret anchoring him in this dimension.

"Do you still have the regrets you came in with?" I asked.

"I may still have some," Charles answered. "But more and more the feeling seems like a splinter that I increasingly understand how to extract."

Charles looked at me with a joyful smile and did a little jig with hands on hips, so for a moment I could see what he must have been like as the twenty-two-year-old sailor with a scraggly jawline beard. "If my life has taught me anything, it is that I do not want to be limited again." Once you have been in this dimension, it is indeed quite a commitment to go back and reexperience the earth plane, not to mention being squished into the body of a baby.

"I often wonder if I knew, as I let go of my hold on the ship's stay ropes, that I would meet my end. I even asked my angels, as they walked me on the path to this dimension, if I did that on purpose," Charles confided. They told Charles that he did not do it on purpose but that intuitively he knew a door was opening and how to go through it so he would be released before the seawater filled his lungs. They said that sometimes one's intuition moves consciousness toward a certain action so a transition can occur. Charles told me that when we no longer fear what is happening to the body, we experience a state of grace as we transition.

During his time here, he had ample opportunity to reflect on his experiences and understand how regret can become integrated with everyday life. Meeting Charles gave me some insight into the meaning and consequences of holding on to thoughts and emotions that don't serve us and keep us separate from choice and freedom.

Editor's note: Miller is a common name, thus there may be no way to identify the gentleman Galen met. Based on a conversation they'd had, however, Galen seemed to think the man was on the Confederate side of the Civil War. In my research, I was able to find a Charles Miller, seaman, Florida Volunteer Coast Guards, mustered in December 15, 1861;

transferred to company K, 7th Florida Infantry, 1862; transferred to the Confederate States Navy, August 5, 1862, as quarter gunner aboard the CSS *Chattahoochee*; also served on the CSS *Savannah*.[1]

Many ships have nicknames, but unless the CSS *Savannah* was nicknamed *Madeline* this was not the Charles Miller that Galen encountered. The CSS *Savannah* did founder in bad weather in August 1863, but it was a gunboat and did not have the rigging Charles described (stays, which are large bundles of ropes supporting the masts and anchored to the sides of the deck). There was a lake schooner named *Madeline* (built in Fairport, Ohio, in 1845) in commercial operation during the years in question, but I could only find references to it sailing on the waters of Lake Michigan.

The dedication to his ship, death at sea, and isolation from his family that Charles Miller described was not an uncommon experience for sailors of the era. No doubt he sent money to his family, but he did not see himself as a husband and father because he was committed to his life at sea. And due to his father's influence on his choice of career, he did not feel that he made the choice himself. Yet in his imagination and in his connection to the natural elements, he experienced another aspect of life that allowed him access to his spirit, reflected in his visions of angels. He was able to connect to the stream of the unified field that flows beneath polarity. In a sense, being at sea removed a lot of distractions from his life, permitting him

---

[1] "Soldiers of Florida," *Robert Watson Diary* (August 5, 1862): ORN 2, 1, 304.

to serve his soul through this connection. His experience was limited, and yet he was a complex man. Survival, duty, and insight were the themes of his life.

I had my own encounter with a sailor of sorts in the mid-1990s. In a dream, I found myself in darkness twelve thousand feet below sea level. A lone man passed in front of me, walking across the corroding deck of a wrecked ship, which I recognized as the RMS *Titanic*. Trailing behind him were several feet of his intestines. I immediately understood he was haunting this vessel because he believed he was responsible for it sinking. An officer, he had had something to do with delivering the message that significant icebergs lay in the path of the RMS *Titanic*. He felt that whatever he said, however, was inadequate to convey the peril the ship was facing. His guilt and self-anger were palpable, but I said to him, "You really weren't responsible for what happened, as there were many reasons this accident took place."

It was clear he felt I had misunderstood the situation and didn't fully appreciate the scope of the tragedy for which he was responsible. So he attempted to show me just how horrible he was by taking me back to that fateful night in 1912, showing me one horrific scene after another. The gore and mayhem became so extreme that it almost seemed like a black comedy, and I laughed at the antics created by this man to convince me he was hideous. Upon awakening, I could tell I had only succeeded in infuriating this ghost, although my hope had been to see him eventually gain perspective and integrate his experiences and feelings of guilt.

This dream sequence made it clear to me how belief structures involving regret and anger can trap the personality in an earthbound dimension pending the emergence of a new level of understanding.

Photo courtesy of Wikimedia Commons

CHAPTER 3

Monica

SHORTLY AFTER I ARRIVED HERE, I became aware of a young woman always standing in the same place in a field, a beautiful willow tree towering in front of her. At all times, she faced the tree with a very large red parrot perched on her shoulder and looking like she was cradling something in her arms. She stood so still it was as if she were a mannequin someone had placed in this position.

One day, out of curiosity I decided to approach her. Drawing closer, I could see her turn her head slightly, fear flashing in her eyes as my legs made a swishy noise against the knee-high grass. I could also see that what she was cradling in her arms was a large cat whose fur gradually changed color from white to silver to black. The red parrot, which towered over the top of her head, never changed color. Both animals acknowledged me as I approached, the parrot stretching its wings a little and making a mute squawk and the cat turning its head toward me.

I noticed that the woman had a pretty face and long brown hair, and that she was shorter than me, about 5 feet 6 inches, although not much older. Her slight fear reminded me of my mother, and I wondered if that had drawn me to her. Her edges were not yet well defined, because she was still trying to become grounded in this dimension, but her body was in sharp focus.

I looked directly into her eyes and said, "Hello."

"Hello," she answered in a friendly manner, though still somewhat reserved.

"The parrot and cat are really lovely. Are they your pets?" I added, trying to break the ice.

"Yes, they were given to me when I came here, in the hope that they would comfort me. At first I was a little afraid of the bird, but those who helped me here said it would protect me, so I learned not to fear it," she replied.

At that moment the parrot squawked loudly, causing her to jump a little and surprising me too, because it was as if the bird had been listening to our conversation. It soon became evident that these companions were not what they appeared to be. Looking into their eyes, I could see the parrot had superb consciousness and the cat was a loving being. During this moment of recognition, the cat gave me a little smile and wink as if he knew what I had discovered. I was aware also that here cats are keepers of secrets. I was sure this woman had no idea yet about the real nature of her companions, just as I had not realized my dog Andy's true nature as a teacher, believing him to be only a dog.

As she often looked past me at the tree, I assumed the woman was new to this dimension and needed time to become grounded, so I gave her space during our first encounter. On another day, when I approached her for a second time, I spoke to her parrot and cat so she would not think I was focused just on her and feel uneasy. On my third visit, I asked her name, and she looked at me as if that was the oddest question I could ask.

"My name?" she replied.

"Yes. My name is Galen," I said. Then to jump-start the conversation, I told her a little about myself—that I loved animals and she somehow reminded me of my mom.

Finally, she blurted out, "My name is Monica Auten."

"I am very glad to meet you, Monica," I answered, and with that she smiled and relaxed a bit. Knowing I could come back and talk to her anytime I wanted, since she was always in the same place, I left things at that for a while.

One day I visited Monica and brought Andy to meet her. As we approached, Andy ran ahead, sniffed her knees, and looked up at the parrot and cat. Immediately Monica came alive, brightening up with Andy there. I realized that I hadn't noticed how sickly pale she had been by comparison. Perhaps the energies of the three animals combined had set off this transformation.

"Hi, Monica. How are you doing today?" I asked as I caught up with Andy.

"I am doing much better," she said, then proceeded to ask me about Andy and how we met, which was not so different from how she had met her animal friends.

"Andy just showed up," I said. "No one in particular gave him to me for protection. He has been with me ever since, for which I am very grateful, because he helps me feel less alone. Andy has a wonderful way of making a person feel better."

"Yes, I noticed," Monica answered.

To find out a little more about Monica, I asked her how she got here.

"I am not sure, but I am glad I am here," she said, her voice cracking. I found that curious because often individuals are not so enthusiastic about being in this dimension.

"Do you understand why you are here?" I asked.

"Yes. I know I am dead. I was murdered," she answered as her throat closed up.

"I am very sorry," I said, curious about the circumstances of her passing but not wanting to insist on details. Andy stood close to her, and the cat and parrot leaned toward her as if to offer support.

After a pause, she began to describe the events surrounding her murder. As she did, I could actually see them; it was as if I were reliving them with her. She told me she had been returning home after shopping when a strange man approached her on the sidewalk. He was taller and much older than she was, and he blocked her path and asked for a cigarette. Explaining that she did not have one, she walked around him. But the next thing she knew, he moved in front of her again and pulled her into his vehicle, where he knocked her unconscious.

Upon regaining a glimmer of consciousness, she could see the scenery out the window of the moving vehicle and, from the position of the sun, she realized that a significant amount of time had gone by. As more time passed and she had fully regained consciousness, she saw she was now in a pitch-black space, cold and damp, with a dirt floor. Reaching out, she could feel the cinder blocks of what had to have been a wall. Then standing on her tiptoes, she tried touching the ceiling to get the dimensions of this room, soon running into a post that supported the ceiling and, nearby, a chair.

Feeling the back of her head where she had been hit, she discovered it was swollen and painful to the touch, and she began to cry, then scream. A balding man in his late forties, who smelled like he had never bathed, suddenly appeared in the doorway, then proceeded to tie her up, rape her, and beat her. Eventually untying her, he talked to her nicely, as if trying to woo her, and left. For what she guessed was several days, she drifted in and out of consciousness in the darkness, hungry and thirsty. The man came back several times to repeatedly rape and beat her, and each time he entered the room she could see, through a crack in the door, a lovely tree off in the distance.

Finally, she felt so demoralized and hurt that she decided to defend herself at any cost the next time he came. She pulled the chair over to the post so she could swing it at him the moment he opened the door and then try to escape. Indeed, the next time he opened the door, she swung the chair at him, but her attack only succeeded in making him mad. He tied her to the post and began punching her in the stomach. Suddenly she felt something inside of her explode, and she doubled over in pain, at which point her tormentor left.

When he came back, she lay dying. She could feel her abdomen swelling and could taste blood in her mouth. She expected him to do his usual routine, but the sight of her caused him to do something unexpected. He untied her, collapsed on the ground next to her, and held her. She could feel his warm tears dropping onto her face just before she slipped out of her body and rose up out of the building, seeing the beautiful tree she had glimpsed so many times from her prison.

"My grandmother met me, and others walked me toward the light of this dimension," she told me. "Standing in the light was a radiant being. It may have been Jesus, I am not sure, but it felt like that kind of love. The being told me there would be no more suffering and gave me this bird and cat for company and protection. They guided me to this place and told me I would heal here."

Since Monica not only described her experiences in those last days of her life but shared her feelings as well, her story touched me deeply.

She looked me in the eyes and said, "You know, everything is going to be okay, and you have helped me quite a bit. But I have to let my family know what happened, so as soon as I am strong enough I am going back home."

I did not want to discourage her emotional rally, due probably to the same strength she had gathered while trying to escape from her tormentor, so I just smiled at her and said, "Good. Your family does need to know what happened." I looked at the parrot and then at the cat, and they both shook their heads no, but not obviously enough for her to sense it. She would need a lot of healing before being able to communicate with her family on earth. I thanked her for sharing her story and said, "Whenever you need a hug, I will give you one, and I want you to know that nobody here will hurt you."

I could not fathom why such a horrible thing had happened to such a beautiful being and why she continued to be so traumatized after her transition. Nor could I determine what she was learning while standing frozen before the tree with her bird and cat. Usually when you make the effort to share your story here, you learn lessons, both in and out of classrooms.

To gain more insight, I went to my teacher. "I met Monica Auten, who shared with me her story about abduction, torture, and death, and yet she stands there looking almost as fractured and bewildered as she probably did on her first day here, with her edges fuzzy," I told him.

My teacher replied: "Her soul is so old that it provides others with opportunities for healing. Unknowingly, you moved to a different dimensional station to meet this woman because she had something important to teach you. She was a fine young woman. She was happy, looked toward her future, and had a family who loved her. The man who perpetrated the acts wanted power and control, but at the same time tried to find someone with whom he could make a connection. At any point he could have let her go, but his ego would not let him.

"When she lay dying next to him, he had a profound realization of what he had done. Because of her death, her tormentor gained a different type of understanding. He abducted no other women after that but drank himself to death because of sorrow. The man learned a hard lesson about control and compassion. So, in a sense, he died because of her and then she became his doorway out of that life.

"She will heal and gather wisdom. She has two very fine teachers with her who will protect her and help her progress. Everything in this dimension is here to help her, but first she has to overcome the trauma."

"Her story seemed so real, as if I had been there," I said, hoping to understand this aspect of our encounter.

"That's because she is still experiencing trauma. She arrived after you did, so for her this is all very new. She still needs to make a connection back into her body and her heart. She desperately wants to let her family know what happened to her, and many individuals are doing their best to inform them that she is okay."

As so often before, the explanation provided by my teacher gave me a better understanding of what had happened to me and of the wider implications death can have for some people.

༄ ༄ ༄

Editor's note: Monica's story reflects the danger of living in a society that exploits sex for profit and power. The media bombards us with images of sex on everything from billboards to computer screens, and computers have made pornography more accessible to people than ever before. I favor free expression, but am concerned about the effect exploitation of sex has on the many disenfranchised malcontents who live on the periphery of society, such as the man who tortured and killed Monica. Women are in danger as a result, and the solution is not for women to walk in fear or have an escort or a taser gun with them at all times, but for us all to remember that only 150 to 200 years have passed since misogyny stopped being a core value in Western society. With increased awareness of this reality, we may discover that some of what we allow in the name of freedom actually puts others at risk.

Attempting to verify Monica's story from historical records, I was able to find a twenty-one-year-old Monica Auten who went missing in Florida in May of 2006 and who fit the description Galen provided, but a call to the Orange County Sheriff's Department revealed that the historical Monica Auten had been located. The person Galen was talking to was clearly not this woman; however, she could have been so broken by her experience that she had confused herself with the Monica who was still alive on earth.

Here is how this may have happened. Individuals representing the victim archetype, such as the Monica whom Galen encountered, can take on bits and pieces of the surrounding environment by essentially fastening to themselves shards of a broken mirror. Others in their social circle, dazzled by the sparkles of reflection from these broken pieces of reality, may get too close and be energetically pricked by the sharp edges, allowing the victim to feed on them while drawn into their drama. In other words, Monica may have "glued" onto herself the persona of the Monica on earth and identified with her.

By way of further clarification, Monica's experience of seeing a Christ-like figure upon arriving seems to illustrate Galen's view that individuals arrive at the other side with their belief systems intact. The Christ-like figure, in this context, reflected Monica's belief system. Galen has explained that the contents of the silver cup, which symbolize an individual's earth experiences, reveal the personality's point of view or belief about those experiences. Evidently, Monica's continuous standing was her way of connecting to her processes, while Galen had connected to his processes by repeatedly creating what was familiar to him until he understood that he did not necessarily have to have what was familiar to him to feel safe and connected. Similarly, Galen was confused about how Monica could still feel so traumatized at his dimensional station, not yet aware that she wasn't at his dimensional station; he was still too new to heaven to know he had dropped down to a dimensional station where traumas are worked out.

Like Galen, I too wondered why Monica remained standing in front of her tree experiencing what appeared to be post-traumatic stress disorder and why she was holding on to the trauma even after she crossed. I began to question how much she had been told upon arrival, as I didn't understand why she would have stood catatonic in front of a tree if she had been given some understanding of why her soul and spirit chose to have this experience. But even if she had been told everything when she arrived, I realized, she would not have been able to integrate it since she first had to integrate herself. There seems to be a form of cognitive restructuring on the other side. Cognitive therapy seeks to help people overcome difficulties by identifying and changing dysfunctional thinking, behavior, and emotional responses. According to cognitive restructuring theory, our unrealistic beliefs are directly responsible for generating dysfunctional emotions and their resultant behaviors.[1] Upon identifying an experience that was not completely understood, and reviewing it from as many different vantage points as necessary, we dismantle the misconceptions driving dysfunctional emotions and reconstruct a more realistic understanding of the experience, and hence a more functional emotional response to that experience.

Viewing Monica's behavior from this perspective, it may be that by standing there catatonic, holding strongly to the role of victim, she was working on her own cognitive restructuring process while simultaneously helping Galen with his and commenting on society. She brought to the fore his compassion to bear witness as he listened to her story and she extended compassion to other victims of abuse by telling it, making it clear that she had been not only an abused woman but also a warrior determined to defend herself no matter what the cost because there was a beautiful tree beyond the door—a symbol of freedom.

Monica's story also reminded me of the book Mark Twain worked on during the last twenty years of his life—*The Mysterious Stranger*—which, although never finished, was published

---

[1] Judith S. Beck, "Questions and Answers about Cognitive Therapy," in *About Cognitive Therapy: Basics and Beyond* (New York: The Guilford Press, 1995).

posthumously. The Satan character in the book points out how the timing of an individual's death reflected the kindest fate for them, given the alternatives they would have had if they had remained on earth. If Monica had survived her ordeal, her psychological trauma may have made the rest of her life very difficult on many levels.

This woman had drawn Galen to her, although he didn't know why. On hearing her story, I remembered that something strikingly similar had happened to Galen's mother before I met her, and I wondered if unresolved issues from her traumatic experience had affected her ability to have a healthy relationship with me. Our relationship, I realized, may have been fractured by a blow that had taken place before we met.

Suspecting that Galen was drawn to Monica because she reminded him of his mother, I wondered if he somehow sensed that his mother had been traumatized like Monica had. To my mind, their meeting did not seem coincidental; after all, not only did Monica look like his mother but she represented a piece of his mother's story that he did not know.

While there were a lot of things about his mother I wanted to share when Galen was alive, opportunities were lacking and he did not yet have the maturity to process the information. During the last six months of his earth life, he wasn't even talking to me and had in fact moved out of my house; but now the opportunity had presented itself so I told Galen this piece of his mother's history. One never wants to hear that someone they love has gone through such a trauma; however, it helped Galen understand why he had been so driven to instinctively take care of his mother. It also helped me realize there was nothing I could have done to save my relationship with her, though I had tried everything I knew of at the time.

A few nights later, in a dream Galen guided me to the attic of the house where he had been born. It was V shaped and above the living room, but I had covered it with drywall and carpeted the floor. The room was empty except for a logbook Galen had left for me to read. I opened the book and saw it was a libretto about my marriage to his mother, as if that period of my life was now just some opera. Going right to the character description of his mother, I learned she had made a conscious decision to hide from me her troubled thoughts and beliefs.

As a result, I received confirmation that had she instead confided in me things would have been different. She would have had the opportunity to release certain patterns, and change would have occurred. But her mistrust of male energy due to her history told her not to trust me. In the end, the information given to me by Galen allowed me to clear the attic of my marriage and to be released from one more piece of guilt. Galen told me he knows I did not abandon his mother or him, and now I know it too, to the core.

Every day, individuals choose not to open up and thus not to provide opportunities for change, largely because of mistrust. I have been told that if one can stand in the crossroads of change and let the guidance of love answer the voice of mistrust, it can be overcome.

CHAPTER 4

Benjamin

My daily routine here often reflects my routine on earth. Like everyone on earth, I was accustomed to sleeping, so at night I still go to bed and in the morning I wake up, grab a bite to eat, and prepare for the day. I have created several living spaces for myself, but my favorite one has the flavor of my home on earth. It has walls, windows, furniture, and even a television to provide familiarity. I tend to use the TV for personal creative purposes rather than as entertainment from an external source, as people do on earth. I can watch anything on the TV I have access to. For example, I can tune in to my father's energy field or view a movie he has watched. I can also use the TV screen to create just as I would have done on a computer while on earth. Although I have not been invited to see the Hall of Records (Akashic Records), called the Hall of Cups, on my TV I can tap in to those who have access to it. This is an informational dimension, and having direct access to these records does not hold the importance it has on earth. On earth, TV programming consists of what other people want you to see, but here I watch what I want to see, according to what I feel like interacting with or creating. This environment offered me a sense of normalcy when I arrived, and still does, but now I am more active in creating and manifesting.

Having the familiar around me has given me a sense of stability that helps me stay centered and feel comfortable reaching out to those around me. This was something I learned to do here, because connecting with individuals was not one of my best skills on earth. But now I love listening to others, especially in classrooms. They are good places to focus attention on teachers and also to observe and connect with others. Because my classmates tend to be at the same level I am, the classroom provides opportunities to watch the learning processes of others and, by comparison, assess my own. Most of us here introduce ourselves by saying, "Hi, how are you? How did you get here?" In this way, we learn about the circumstances and deaths of our fellow classmates.

As I have become better at engaging fully with the energy and individuals around me, I have found more and more people who shared my experience of leaving the body very quickly, although not always because of an accident. For instance, while attending class I encountered four individuals who were there because of an accident that had caused them to leave their bodies while efforts were being made to keep them alive, as well as a man named Benjamin who had died abruptly.

Benjamin, who appeared to be in his thirties, said in a nondescript midwestern accent, "I had a very unexpected heart attack. I felt dizzy and began to bleed from both my nose and my mouth. Next thing I knew, I was dead."

In the normal course of events when leaving the body, teachers, family, and friends of the deceased will escort the individual to this dimension, but that was not the case for Benjamin. Feeling that his body had betrayed him by giving out on him without warning, and wanting to know why, he stayed with his body throughout his autopsy, where he learned that an aneurysm on his aorta had ruptured. The problem might have been caught on a routine chest X-ray earlier in his life, but as he was relatively young and had no symptoms he had never been X-rayed.

After his family had him cremated, he remained on the earth plane without an anchor and decided to communicate with his family. He visited his siblings and parents in their homes, staring directly into their faces. Some family members could sense him standing there, but they were not comfortable interacting emotionally with a being who had no physical body.

At first, Benjamin found there was a certain novelty in being a disembodied spirit, then he started to panic. Although he sometimes got reactions, no one made a connection to him except for grieving their loss of him. Also, he wondered why he'd never encountered a tunnel of light or a helper after he had left his body—the experiences he'd heard take place when individuals die.

One day as he sat alone on a park bench feeling sad about being stuck in a dimension to which he no longer belonged, he saw a woman staring at him from a bench across the way, actually able to see him. He walked over to her, and with eyes reflecting kindness she introduced herself as Marcy and said, "You need to go into the light now."

Immediately, he was transported to the other side and found himself walking with his teacher, who explained what had happened and handed him his silver cup. He was grateful that Marcy had the skill and perception to help him continue on his path. Without her, he said he would have been lost due to his stubbornness and curiosity about why he had died.

Benjamin told me part of the reason he had become trapped on earth was due to society's lack of awareness about life's processes. He said that in certain eras and cultures, time was allowed to elapse after an individual passed to give the body a chance to completely release the spirit. It was recognized that not all spirits leave immediately, and through prayer, or chanting, an effort was made to guide the spirit forward.

However, he added, the fascination that caused him to stay with his body during the autopsy had allowed him to learn that it had not really betrayed him. He realized that the human body is made of matter, and matter is to be respected and cared for, because it is our vessel in the third dimension. After learning that his body had not betrayed him, he had forgiven it and been able to start integrating his experiences.

I was very interested in Benjamin's story because my experience was so different. At the time I passed, I was presented with a choice, whether to stay or leave, even though my personality was not privy to the particulars at that moment. While I could have stayed with my physical body, I would have chosen to remain with it only if I did not yet want to move forward. In that case, I would have been a quadriplegic, and while many individuals have chosen to learn and serve from such an experience, that would not have been my situation had I remained.

As soon as I transitioned to the other side, my teacher showed up, but for Benjamin, who died among his family, his shock and anger about what had happened kept him from hearing the beings who would have ushered him forward. Even so, he had a valuable experience and vowed he would use this information to help others upon his return to earth. Perhaps he'll teach about the importance of understanding what takes place around the physical body immediately after death. Just as birth is different from one individual to the next, so too is death.

Editor's note: Benjamin's story is not uncommon, since many people get stuck in the ethers. After my father passed, he was stuck wandering around his house, ignored by his wife, but he was not as perceptive as Benjamin. My father just thought he was having another bad day. I discussed in *My Life after Life* how the guides who come through the trance medium Audrey Wrinkles walked me through a visualization during which I brought my father the piece he needed to reconnect with his helpers—a crystal bowl of water into which I urged him to look. He never saw me but instead saw one of his older sisters holding this bowl, which was all that he required to be set free. I think my father got stuck because of his belief system, according to which individuals who die are dead, as in gone forever. Thus when he found himself conscious he believed he must still be alive in his physical body on earth. Benjamin, on the other hand, identified with his body so strongly he was furious with it for failing him but quickly found out he was not his body. Our society is quick to judge people by their bodies rather than recognizing the beings who occupy them.

The only person I know who could have done what Marcy did for Benjamin is the author Joan Grant (1907–1989), who discussed such activities in her book *Many Lifetimes*, which she coauthored with her husband, Dr. Denys Kelsey. For her, the veil between the worlds did not exist.

Benjamin's story is a reminder that the human body is frail and does not take well to abuse. As a physician, I can say with some confidence that the human body should be able to thrive for at least 120 years if cared for appropriately—body, mind, and spirit—and then die healthy of old age, but I know of no one who has experienced this outcome. Even if we have not physically abused our bodies through hard labor or the elective poisons of poor quality food, alcohol, or tobacco, we abuse them unconsciously through poisons we permit in our environment, such a fluoride, aspartame, mercury, vaccines, dental amalgams, and pesticides. We allow ourselves to be experimented on with too much ease, and unless we incarnate with a great deal of protection from those in higher dimensions, as well as our loved ones here on earth, coming to this beautiful planet is a gamble played out by the soul.

CHAPTER 5

Arthur and Eileen

THIS IS A BUSY DIMENSIONAL STATION with many comings and goings, yet at the same time it is very pastoral. There are opportunities to change numerous aspects of the environment, so there is a lot of transformation. Most of the residents are purposefully involved with their studies and other activities to help them advance along their paths. Some individuals seem to be a consistent part of the scenery. Whether walking along a sidewalk, gardening, or painting their fences, they give the impression that they have always been here. Although most of the teachers have also been here a long time, these other individuals have a different vibration that appears to steady the energy around them. Their function seems to be to model certain types of behavior, unlike the role teachers have of creating educational experiences so individuals can understand universal laws and truths. For example, one very cute older couple always walk arm in arm no matter what they are doing, looking like the epitome of grandparents. They seem to exemplify love, connectedness, and stability. I smile every time I see them, as their enjoyment of each other is infectious and reassuring.

I have approached them, but they do not want to talk. The man, who wears a white shirt and khaki pants, will tip his hat a little but keeps walking with his partner, who is dressed in a lavender pantsuit. Sometimes I have gotten a "good morning" out of them, but they never stop to engage in conversation. Even so, I don't feel that they have ever given me the brush-off either.

Curious about their behavior, I asked my teacher about them.

"Arthur and Eileen, which is what we call them, have always looked exactly as they do now, and they have always behaved exactly as they do now. Likely they will still be here long after you have decided to continue on your journey," he said. My teacher went on to explain that their work here is to impart a feeling of love, contentment, and commitment to everyone who meets them, modeling universal truths. Consequently those who come to this dimensional station from a planet where holding hands may not be part of a courtship ritual still sense how love, contentment, and commitment can be experienced with others. In this way, Arthur and Eileen are ambassadors who weave beautiful threads of universal truth through this dimension. Their contribution engenders exactly what I felt when I first arrived here—a pervasive sense of belonging and peace.

Unlike individuals here who can't wait to get back to earth, Arthur and Eileen's apparent satisfaction in working here to project universal truths to others inspires me. They illustrate that the truth of who we are is more important than any achievements we may strive for. Their compassionate and loving interactions also reflect what sometimes cannot be seen in the families and societies we come from. In many earth societies, the elderly are not respected and people don't understand the importance of acknowledging others with graciousness, like the simple tip of a hat.

Gradually I have become more aware of others who, like Arthur and Eileen, embody universal truths in order to teach others. While Andy functioned this way for me personally—modeling groundedness to help me integrate into this dimension—these others embody universal truths for the entire dimension. For instance, there is a woman who goes out every day and paints, embodying creative energy. Likewise, there is a man who whistles and keeps his hands in his pockets as he walks, embodying freedom and happiness. And there are individuals who are in no hurry and have no agenda. All are simply part of this environment, and others learn through their example.

Like Arthur and Eileen, these people hold a vibrational space. You can sometimes engage them in a casual conversation, though rarely one with any depth. And because we can use our imaginations to layer over the events taking place, beings who are doing the same type of work as Arthur and Eileen, or the painter or whistler, may at times go unnoticed.

I asked another teacher if these beings had ever been incarnate. He explained that they represent what is left over after a soul incarnates for the last time on a lower dimensional planet. Because their last incarnation was powerful and centered, some go on to be recognized as avatars, mahatmas, or saints. Having changed the vibration of the world they inhabited, when they pass from their bodies they do not return to this dimension as a whole entity; rather, a piece of their soul separates and shares its experiences and intentions with a multitude of others, mostly in the soul family from which it came. So much of what we see walking around are apsects of great souls holding vibrations, with no need to incarnate again since a piece of them has seeded itself with souls who are still incarnating.

These aspects of the great souls here hold a form with no other purpose. They live with memories but don't share information because they are neither teachers nor healers, but dedicated archetypes for this dimension. It is not that they don't care about individuals enough to participate; it is simply that they have no agenda. The aspects with agendas separated from them to be utilized by others.

Editor's note: The individuals Galen describes project wonderful energy, but I told him I was not convinced they were anything more than the Divine holding a frequency that supported the infrastructure of the dimension. I called them "sentinels,"

because by their presence they are guarding the vibrations of what they symbolize in that space. They are energy fields maintaining the best of humanity's attributes.

The other side, according to Galen, is a dimensional realm consisting of numerous levels suspended in some form of photonic reality that, in part, is held together by nodes of energy moving through it. Level 21, where Galen resides, is the highest level that still holds the faintest shadow of the earth plane. It resembles an intimate college-like town with an expansive greenbelt where the sentinels exist as a reminder that this is a created space somewhere and yet nowhere at all. Our spirits may be merely aspects of the Divine in the eternal pursuit of perfection.

If our realities are created, as they seem to be, the source of the creation is too expansive and powerful to be ignored. In fact, striving to understand the source is ultimately behind any attempt at a coherent explanation of our dimension. An interesting explanation for why we exist here is to have experiences in a frequency lacking the pervasive sense of knowingness and belonging that is found elsewhere.

Not knowing the mysteries of the universe now bothers me. In particular, not understanding our relationship to Source—the how and why of who we are—increasingly affects my communication with my son and my understanding of his location. Reason and logic are survival tools we have been given to understand our dimension, but understanding Source is beyond reason and logic; and while my personality is not satisfied with that reality, it also knows there is no point arguing about it.

Galen's explanation of the individuals who represent archetypes clarifies why certain people feel they were historic personalities, such as Joan of Arc. Everyone who thinks they may have been Joan of Arc could be partially correct, even though none of them was Joan of Arc but just picked up on a piece of the great soul being distributed throughout its soul family after that incarnation. When I asked Galen what might have happened to the real Joan of Arc, he said the part of her soul that was not distributed could have become a sentinel, perhaps taking on a form reflecting the archetype that soul was working to support and bearing no resemblance to the soul's role during that incarnation.

Another example of one of these great souls might be Mahatma Gandhi, but if so the part of the soul remaining would not have the appearance of a man sitting cross-legged, wearing a dhoti, and creating homespun thread, as his soul would have taken on an appearance to suit the archetype it was working to exemplify. On the other hand, today's Dalai Lama is an aspect of a soul chosen to incarnate over and over again because of an agreement to carry forward a tradition and teach from a particular form, even though that soul has matured past the earth experience. Although each Dalai Lama is not exactly like the last, because upon leaving every succeeding incarnation, part of that soul disperses outward, what returns still has enough memory of previous incarnations to carry on with that lineage and service. Then, too, souls who graduate from lower dimensions have multiple options available to them, only one of which is to become a sentinel in a higher dimension.

For any soul, returning to earth is not about checking off a list of requirements and then graduating; rather, it reflects the soul's choice, and there is great enthusiasm among many to return to the earth plane, generally conceived as a place where all memory of where one came from and where one is going is veiled. But there are also souls who, having matured beyond the earthly dimension, desire to come back and experience being incarnate with full awareness and understanding of where they came from and where they are going. In addition, it is possible to have experiences without utilizing birth and death cycles, as many evolved beings have never incarnated.

Ultimately, a soul does not have to graduate from the earth plane to choose a more advanced avenue of experience. Nor does an individual require the fame of a Joan of Arc or a Gandhi to graduate from the earth plane. Evolving is more about completing one's understanding of the lessons earth has to offer and making a contribution, as it has been for Arthur and Eileen.

CHAPTER 6

Sally

JUST AS MULTIPLE LEVELS OF REALITY EXIST together on earth, they do in my dimension as well, only here they are far more discrete. Even so, one level is no grander than another, and no one is more special simply because they are here rather than on earth.

An individual is put at a certain level on the basis of their experiences, not their religious beliefs. Of greatest importance are experiences demonstrating the person's ability to operate from the heart—with openness, awareness, and a sense of interconnectedness. Some levels here concern healing for those who have had a very limited earth experience due, for example, to addiction, such as alcoholics or individuals psychologically addicted to a behavior pattern, like needing to have the newest material thing. Although such people may not have richness of experience when they pass, the opportunity for expansion is always available in this dimension. And the more expansive an individual's experience is on earth, the more resources they have to work with here.

On earth there is an illusion regarding the fate of individuals in the afterlife. Many people believe that if they live good, conservative lives on earth they will end up in a place referred to as heaven. However, it is the ability to be open and willing to participate in life that brings individuals to a place of expanded possibilities here.

At my dimensional station, everyone I meet exhibits openness. Even Monica, after moving past her trauma, arrived at my dimensional station because she had lived with openness, although she could not use this quality to overcome imprisonment by her captor. If ten years of openness, awareness, and connectedness is part of someone's experience, an event that causes bitterness or fear, closing the person down, cannot eradicate their former experience. In life, experiences are kept as if in a bank, then later go into the silver cup we are all given upon arrival here. Even one moment of loving your neighbor will give you the chance to expand and grow. In fact, love and compassion are never wasted; all such experiences are utilized at some point.

A woman I met here, who is nothing like me, nevertheless helped me better understand the meaning of these ideas. Meeting her seemed curious at first because, while I have always attracted the familiar around me, she looked exactly like a bag lady. I have since realized that as I become less rigid in my ideas about people here, much more diversity becomes available to me.

This woman had gray, matted hair, stained, worn clothes, and was pushing a grocery cart filled with bags containing an assortment of things. My first thoughts were: "How did she get here?" and "I wonder if she's crazy." But I just said, "Hello."

"Oh, you are an angel," the woman answered.

Her eyes were the lightest, clearest blue I had ever seen. Her hair may have been matted and tangled as it trailed down her back, but what showed in her was pure light. I was drawn to her with such an emotional force that I nearly cried when I looked in her face. I asked her to tell me about herself.

"My name is Sally, and I am not sure how I got here. When I arrived, it was explained that I had died, but I was never aware of my death. I never understood how one moment I was there and in the next people were welcoming me, explaining who I am, and guiding me. But it doesn't matter, as I am so happy here. I was happy where I used to be as well. I loved everybody and enjoyed the excitement of living every day on the street." She went on to say that, despite her excitement, many people ignored her, never returning her greetings. She had a special talent when incarnate: the ability to see the spirits of others and thus determine whether their hearts were open. When she recognized in their faces the same light I was seeing in her face, she would call them angels.

After hearing her story and considering her perspective on life, despite her dismal appearance I was very taken by her. She spoke clearly of simple ideals, to the point that I began to wonder if she was a teacher.

"What was the last thing you remember before you got here?" I asked, hoping to understand more about her circumstances in this dimension.

"I remember being in front of a pawn shop and a man offering me a drink out of a little bottle—I liked drinking and drank it. Then I remember lying down and going to sleep, and when I woke up I was pushing my cart somewhere else, joined by two beings who told me that I had passed out of my body and was now here, safe, not being judged."

She laughed and told me she appreciated not being judged in this dimension because in her life she had always liked releasing others from their judgmental attitudes, although she knew it was not her soul's assignment. "I kept my form because in many ways it protected me on earth. It was also a sort of window that helped me see into the hearts of others according to how they reacted to me. It wasn't about whether they gave me money but rather whether their eyes reflected an open heart," she explained.

Then she showed me a few items in her cart and asked me how I got here and if I had family. After I shared my story with her, she asked me the most interesting question: "So how do you like living here?"

I had never really thought about this, so I answered simply, "I'm fine here."

I realized that my inability to answer Sally's question more fully was because I felt that if I said I loved it here I would somehow be betraying my earth life, including my family and friends. Here I was free to be in touch with all the layers of self—my heart, mind, body, soul, and spirit. But I also was carrying within me a kind of shame, something I hadn't realized before.

Sally just smiled at me with her clear blue eyes and luminescent face and said, "Maybe you should think about that for a while to see if you can be comfortable enough here to be completely yourself."

Then she laughed and said she had a lot of things to do and should be going. As I watched her pushing her cart down the sidewalk, I wondered how she had zeroed in on the fact that, despite everything I had been learning at this dimensional station, I had not yet fully committed to being here. Beyond that, the story of her life had helped me understand the importance of experiencing love for people despite their circumstances in life.

Editor's note: Unfortunately, the closing of mental health hospitals across the United States in the 1970s created a class of shunned individuals, including homeless bag ladies like Sally, on the streets of many cities. With her open heart and expanded perspective on life, if Sally had lived somewhere on earth with appropriate nourishment, health care, and support, her life might have progressed differently. Perhaps her gift of seeing into the hearts of others would have blossomed into more of a service to others as opposed to being strictly a tool for her personal survival. She might have lived a powerful life instead of dying of perhaps hypothermia or a heart attack in her sleep after having one drink too many.

Just as Galen's meeting with Sally debunked the illusion people have on earth that living a good life will get them to a certain place in the afterlife, it also cast light on the illusion of entitlement. In a sense, we are all guests here on earth because sooner or later we will be leaving. When I am a guest in someone's home, I go out of my way to be respectful and to contribute in exchange for the opportunity to share their space; certainly, I don't act like I own the place by raiding the kitchen and trashing my room. But unfortunately that is what most of us do on this planet. It is regrettable that when incarnating on earth and going through the process of forgetting who we really are and where we came from, manners are forgotten as well.

I don't know if I want to come back to earth, given the level of insanity still present in our immature civilization. But if my soul decides to return, I would like to know I was invited back as a welcome guest.

CHAPTER 7

Mr. Montpelier

One day I was sitting in a classroom of twenty-five students, which was unusual because class size is normally only six or seven, although the rooms are expandable to accommodate as many students as necessary. The teacher was going over a few points I had heard before, so, I am embarrassed to say, I started looking around the room rather than paying attention to her.

In the row behind me, I noticed a gentleman whose leg seemed to be bent at a ninety-degree angle that was not anatomically possible, and I thought, "That is an interesting trick." I was also intrigued by the fact that he was wearing spats over black shoes as a fashion statement, in contrast to his casual attire consisting of jeans and a simple corduroy jacket over a white shirt.

When the class ended and I observed the man hobbling out, I saw that his leg was actually twisted around at a ninety-degree angle and was not the result of how he had been sitting. Curious about his circumstances, I followed him to a tree, where he sat down in the shade. Introducing myself, I said cheerfully, "Hi, I'm Galen. I saw you in class. Did you enjoy the lecture?"

He struggled to get to his feet, extended his hand in a very formal way, and said, with an air of sophistication, "Hello, my name is Mr. Montpelier. I am glad to know you, Galen. If you don't mind, I am going to sit back down. You are welcome to join me."

"I have never seen anyone wear spats here," I commented, hoping he would tell me his story.

"Yes, I like my spats and wore them quite often when I was on earth. I was a very well-to-do man. I enjoyed investing in anything that would make me money, though my favorite investments were diamonds. However, one terrible day I, along with many others, lost all my money, and I identified so much with money and image that I threw myself out of a window, jumping to my death."

I then shared with Mr. Montpelier my knowledge of what individuals who had killed themselves had to go through after becoming trapped in a separate place.

Shaking his head in agreement, he said: "Absolutely. I had to go through that process. When you take your own life, there has to be some reminder left, not as a punishment but as an aid to changing what led to suicide, which is why my leg remains twisted. I agreed to keep my leg the way it was after I jumped out the window, as a reminder that I allowed something to control me other than my respect for love, my excitement at being a seeker, and even my ability to help others. Finally, when it came time for me to move to another level I chose this one because I wished to continue expanding and growing.

"In my life on earth, before becoming fixated on money I focused on expanding my perspective and knowledge. My money at that time allowed me to travel and experience different cultures and ways of living. Instead of staying at fancy hotels or visiting tourist sites, I would meet with wise men, enthralled as I was by the occult. I also tried to understand the spirit world, although I was limited by the spiritualism of my day. It has taken me a while to get to where I am now, but I am grateful for the process because it required me to become very clear about truth and illusion."

Mr. Montpelier went on to say that he will someday reappear on earth but as of now he is not yet ready, adding, "I am planning to first study probabilities that can happen on earth so that I can assist others whose identity is tied to money and also those having financial difficulty. I can't help them all, but maybe those I do help can then assist others. I am deeply dedicated to helping in whatever way I can."

I responded, "I know there are teachers and guides who offer assistance, so I understand what you are saying, but how would you be able to help? How do you change from being a person who committed suicide to one who can assist others?"

Mr. Montpelier replied: "It will happen according to my agreement. If I had remained on earth, I would have become a teacher helping to rebuild the financial stability of the country; but because I got caught up in selfishness I diverted my journey. Now I will continue with my agreement to work as a teacher and guide. Reclaiming who I am is part of my recovery. I am grateful for this chance to continue my journey with others, but to do so I will need to communicate better so that when I connect with them by entering their dreams it doesn't cause me frustration, self-judgment, or disillusionment. I realize, too, that such work will likely involve being disrespected and misinterpreted until I persuade others of the value of my message. I am convinced that the only way to find balance is to remove illusions about money and the fear of losing it. The time will come in the history of humankind for the illusory importance of money to be dispelled and for humans to focus instead on the heart chakra."

Editor's note: The dramatic stock market crash that led to Mr. Montpelier's suicide occurred on "Black Tuesday," October 29, 1929. Between October 29 and November 13, the day stock prices hit their lowest point, the Dow Jones Industrial Average (DJIA) dropped 35 percent, although it recouped nearly all the loss over the next five months. The crash has been blamed for the Great Depression, but that is not the whole story. There have been other sharp drops in the DJIA without an ensuing depression. For example, the DJIA lost a full 45 percent from its January 1973 peak to its October 1974 low, with no ensuing depression, and in October 1987 there was a one-day decline of 508 points, or 23 percent, which took fifteen months to be reversed and also did not result in a depression. The Great Depression probably had more to do with tight credit, austere government spending, and the creation of leverage-based investment (Ponzi) trust schemes by large financial institutions.

Fast forward to recent events in which private banks encouraged subprime lending as far back as 1992 so they could profit from selling toxic mortgages. Organized greed always defeats disorganized democracy, and indeed, financial institutions have been allowed to grow beyond the point of no return, creating trouble around the globe just so they can profit from the fallout. They don't care who gets hurt, as long as they profit. These priests of money, the "banksters"—or "globalists," as some call them—have always been an integral part of the government since it came to power after World War II. But now, for the first time they, along with the World Trade Organization, have destabilized the global economy rather than just that of the United States.

Because polarity, the operational paradigm on earth, is like a rubber band that when stretched beyond a certain point will correctively snap back, it is no surprise to hear from Mr. Montpelier that there may come a time when the nature of commerce and trade will change to the point where the illusions surrounding money will dissipate, an event that is already beginning to take place. It is conceivable that the importance of money will be relegated to history and perhaps money as we now know it will cease to be used.

The historical research I undertook revealed no information about a Mr. Montpelier, but I did learn that in 1929 the commodities exchange also took a very big hit, and since the United States represented 80 percent of the market for polished diamonds, the demand for them plummeted virtually to zero. So if Mr. Montpelier had invested most of his money in diamonds, he would have known rather quickly that he was heading for financial disaster.

Today, it is sometimes regarded as only a myth that individuals working on Wall Street took their own lives by jumping out of windows. There is apparently no official record that anyone did so, but truth often lies behind myths. Interestingly, Winston Churchill, a credible source who was visiting New York during the 1929 Stock Market Crash, wrote the following about the morning after Black Tuesday, when he was awakened by a noisy crowd outside the Savoy Plaza Hotel: "Under my very window a gentleman cast himself down fifteen stories and was dashed to pieces, causing a wild commotion and the arrival of the fire brigade."

Regarding Mr. Montpelier's intention to return to earth to teach and guide others overly focused on money and investments, such transitions can be limited in some ways by suicide. Galen has told me that individuals succumbing to suicide have no choice about the timeline for their return to earth. This is not punishment any more than when someone who cuts off their right arm would be denied a spot on the varsity tennis team.

To understand the limitations resulting from suicide more clearly, consider the following scenario: Visualize a suicidal individual taking a bus to a certain destination. If the person commits suicide by jumping out of the bus before reaching that destination, they would not be able to transfer to another bus line to get back on the road to the planned destination. Instead, they would have to wait for a vehicle in the same bus line to come back and pick them up, but that bus may take time to come around. Regardless of timing, Mr. Montpelier's desire to be a guide and teacher, even though his efforts might not be respected, indicates the sort of learning and growth that occurs on the other side.

Unlike Mr. Montpelier, who jumped to his death out of a sense of hopelessness, some people end their earth life more strategically, in an act of defiance. Such was the case of German trial lawyer Hans Litten.

Hans Achim Litten (June 19, 1903–February 5, 1938) represented opponents of the Nazis, defending the rights of workers during the Weimar Republic between 1929 and 1932. During a trial in 1931, Litten subpoenaed Adolf Hitler to appear as a witness and consequently cross-examined him for three hours, which may have been the only time Hitler was grilled in court by a lawyer. So perturbed was Hitler by the exposure of his agenda to overthrow the existing government that years later he would not allow Litten's name to be mentioned in his presence and, on the night of the Reichstag Fire, had him arrested along with other progressive lawyers and leftists. Litten spent the rest of his life in a series of Nazi concentration camps, enduring torture and interrogations conducted for the sole purpose of humiliating him and breaking his spirit. After five years and a move to Dachau, he committed suicide.

Litten's suicide infuriated many in the Third Reich, and in fact it was a deliberate act of defiance done to beat the Nazis at their own game. Litten remained extremely perceptive about the nature of the world and retained hope at the end. Surely his agenda had been to walk a very difficult path because of the growth and change it promoted and the assistance and advocacy it allowed him to give to others. As on earth, appearances in Galen's dimension are deceiving, and while on the one hand Litten was a suicide, on another his death, unlike Mr. Montpelier's, was not the result of despair and hopelessness. Therefore, Litten's experience on the other side would be very different from Mr. Montpelier's.

Hans Litten
(1903–1938)

CHAPTER 8

The Tsunami Family

I HAVE BECOME INCREASINGLY USED TO the rhythm and patterns of this dimension. In fact, I am far more familiar with the life I have here than my life on earth.

The contrasts between the two dimensions have become quite clear to me. Much on the earth dimension concerns polarity and disconnectedness, while this dimension is about connectedness in a unified field. On earth there is a lot of noise and confusion resulting from the mind's constant thinking, which more often than not gets in the way of discerning between the real and unreal. Also, individuals are forever trying to control situations to obtain goals associated with material concerns. On earth I was almost always thinking about what I was going to do and how I was going to *make* it happen. Here, instead of trying to orchestrate outcomes I can be tranquil and open to what the day may bring. As a result, I am more relaxed and therefore have more opportunities.

One of these opportunities has been to observe a family who had a completely different experience on earth from the others I have described, since they did not live in the United States or grow up white. The family is Asian, likely Thai, and consists of a mother, father, and three children—a boy about fifteen, a boy about eight, and a girl about six—all of whom left the earth on the day of the 2004 tsunami in Thailand. Although they do not speak English, language differences are not a barrier here since we communicate through intention and vibration. So I can understand completely what they are saying, even though I sometimes have to adjust my vibration, like tuning in a radio station.

How this family observes its environment and connects is very different from the behavior of most individuals I have met here. They are all highly aware of their surroundings, and as a result the children seem to have wisdom. Deeply respectful of their environs, they have an acute awareness of the space they occupy and in relation to others. They come to classes but keep to themselves out of a sense of politeness. They have made me examine whether I might be overly friendly or perhaps intruding across others' boundaries and reminded me that not everyone shares my pace and rhythm.

Another thing I love about them are the outfits they wear. I wear a T-shirt, jeans, and tennis shoes so often that it has become my uniform, but this family enjoys dressing creatively, in different styles and colors. You never know what they will be wearing on any given day. I remember one morning the father wore a tuxedo, the mother a polyester pantsuit straight out of the 1970s, and the children brightly colored rumba shirts with ruffles running up and down the sleeves.

I have never asked this family questions, as they don't seem to be interested in conversing. When I talked to my teacher about this, he said it was not because of their culture but because of their traumatic experience of being swept away by the tsunami and dying within a short time of one another and then meeting up on the path to this dimensional station. Because they have a very strong belief in Divine punishment, they think they died together to pay back an old family debt. This is a perfect example of how people's earthly beliefs can still influence them at this dimensional station. It's interesting to be around individuals who were not taught to fear death and learned they would need to exchange energy—family debt, in this case.

Although assured that no family debt had brought them here and that they will not be punished, the family still believes they are paying back a debt since individuals believe what they want to here, where belief is an aspect of freedom. In a sense, this family is working to free the whole human family of its debt—a belief that seems to intensify the separation they maintain from everyone else here. While they appear to have created their own exclusive circle rather than interact with others superficially, they radiate so much beauty and positive energy that they are delightful to be around.

I understand the urge to pay back a perceived debt, because I have similar feelings about contributing to my own family's growth. It is not about sacrifice, but more about gratitude and utilizing situations to their fullest in this dimension to help others. This family illustrates the fact that at the source of the many diverse beliefs on earth is the understanding and love that all people share, which is true as well in this realm.

Perhaps one of the greatest contrasts between the two dimensions is that while holding a cultural belief on earth can separate people from one another, here beliefs can only separate people from their own creative energy. Over time, the beliefs of this family will certainly be better balanced with their creative energy. This is obvious to me because underneath any cultural differences that lead to limiting beliefs are positive human traits: gratitude for family, willingness to do anything for them, and joy for being a part of this effort. So many insights can be gained here simply from observing people's actions.

Editor's note: I have always felt we should have the depth of connection to one another suggested by the scene in *Star Wars* in which Obi-Wan Kenobi felt a very perceptible change in The Force when the Death Star destroyed the planet Alderaan. Consequently, it bothered me that after celebrating Christmas Day 2004 at my mother's house in Los Angeles, Galen and I slept peacefully while on the other side of the world a quarter of a million people lost their lives during the tsunami in Thailand.

After Galen passed, I remembered a dream sequence I had had during the early hours of that December day. I was in the body of a boy about twelve years of age. By his dress I assume he was Tamilian, living in southern India or Sri Lanka. He was joking with a peer about their prepubescent fascination with breasts, but later, while walking alone on the beach near his home, he saw a wall of water coming from an unexpected direction and felt his best chance to survive was to dive underneath it.

After diving, he was tossed about in the frothy violence. Soon things went dark and quiet until I felt a feminine force pulling this lifeless boy out of the water. Then somehow his body was transformed to that of a twenty-nine-year-old man with a cognitive impairment sweeping the floor of a ramshackle cantina. As the boy became conscious of being in the body of an older man with diminished mental capacity, he cried, feeling that his life had been stolen from him.

My role was as an empathic witness to the boy's transition. I did not provide him with any comfort or insight. All I could feel was the impact of the wave that hit him, and how he had been thrown about only to land in a place where he felt trapped.

My first waking thought was that apparently not everyone who died in the tsunami crossed over. I also understood how natural disasters that sweep thousands of lives away in a moment help bring out compassion in others that leads to humanitarian action. While that is a worthwhile thing to do, it does not seem like a satisfactory answer to me. If a quarter of a million souls agreed to open the world's heart on a different level, even if that meant leaving earth themselves, it is a great act of compassion that I don't think a human mind can comprehend. Most humans don't fully understand that there is a continuum of life until they find themselves on the other side and are shown what they just accomplished. If individuals knew they could participate in a realm of connectedness and limitless opportunity to learn and grow, why would they give a second thought to leaving the earth plane, except for ties to beloved family and friends?

The tsunami provided opportunities not only for compassion but for awareness of the earth as having its own evolutionary process. Foundations are changing, and awareness of these alterations is very important for our relationship to the earth in the future.

To further clarify Galen's comments about family, it should be said that Galen loves all members of his family. He and I had a misunderstanding during his last six months on earth, during which time I almost never saw him or had any communication from him, but that was the story of our personalities, not our souls. After Galen crossed over, I remembered that he had come to me in dreamtime when he was thirteen years old and told me he would be leaving. I asked him if he wanted me to go with him, but he was emphatic that I should not follow him, that this was something he had to do alone. He didn't tell me why he had to do it or exactly when but indicated that it would be soon. The rest of our conversation was buried deep in my subconscious mind, apparently a handy closet for spirit to utilize on earth if it doesn't want the personality to find out about something. At some point I had pried open the door to my subconscious mind enough to let out this memory. At the time, my personality was not happy about Galen leaving; from his perspective, however, there was no sacrifice involved in entering a reality of such vast creativity and possibilities for learning. After all, this is where he was in his earth life, old enough to consciously embrace life with all the hopes and dreams of anyone else his age.

Galen is so outgoing and so interested in assisting others to understand the truths that have been revealed to him that it didn't take him long to discover he could teach from his current dimension and thus began working with me to tell his story. My precious son used the curiosity, innocence, and energy that only a teenager can have to open up opportunities for his family to participate in a more conscious manner with life on earth and, in a limited way, with his dimension, where anything is possible, and in so doing transformed us all. The sad fact is that hopelessness can creep into the thoughts of adults because of the cruelty, oppression, poverty, war, and corruption that are present on earth. So there was value in his leaving when he did, and if that is how he understands it, then his leaving cannot be perceived as a sacrifice. But here on earth, where I don't yet see what he can see, I still experience pain regarding his inability to live the life his family expected him to have on earth, even though part of me is glad he didn't have to endure the difficult years of adulthood before gaining the wisdom he now has. During his life on earth, Galen was empathic, sensitive, and refined, and I had many concerns about how he would navigate through his adult years with his delicate butterfly wings. In some ways, I envy the opportunity he now has to learn in his dimension while I continue to sustain challenges regarding his passing as well as my own life.

In commenting on the Thai family he encountered, Galen pointed out that one can walk a path for one's lineage or family. From a more expansive perspective, it can be said that both his actions and the family's contribute to the whole agreement of souls strung together through similar spiritual DNA.

Further, Galen's encounter with this family serves as a reminder to me that his dimensional station is like a global village—actually, a galactic village—although his stories in this book focus on prior earth inhabitants. It is estimated that more than 150,000 people worldwide die every day, so I have questioned why his dimension is a tiny village, like a small college town during summer recess. Galen said he is still gathering information about what is around him and that eventually all levels will be accessible to him as an observer. As he continues to learn and expand, he will gain further awareness of the nature of the levels, but for now he is in a corridor of experience, learning through observation and conversations with various teachers.

When he told me this part of his story, Galen had not yet looked over the horizon to find out just how large his realm is. But he eventually did travel dimensionally through the different levels, as do all individuals who hold the teacher archetype.

CHAPTER 9

The Travelers

I HAVE BARELY BEGUN TO EXPERIENCE LIFE HERE. It's important to state that I don't have omnipotent knowledge just by being in this dimension. I am still continuing to gain knowledge from conversations with my teacher; already I have learned that I will acquire much more knowledge and experience, so much that it seems I will be here for a very long time, although, of course, there is no linear time here. This book project has allowed me to share the knowledge I am increasingly gaining in this realm. It started after I was able, in dreamtime, to introduce my father to those hungry ghosts I call "the travelers," shadowy beings from another universe who feed from humans lacking awareness. Their presence on the earth plane became the impetus for starting the Death Walker series.

I bring up the subject of the travelers realizing some people will misunderstand what I am describing and fall back on superstition. In fact, there are individuals who will not understand the conversation I am having with my father and view it as evil; in their belief systems, I would be considered a demon. But I am also aware that it is important to tell the stories of former earth residents and what they are processing in this dimension, including how some of their belief systems affect their experiences.

In the past when travelers found the energy pattern that could sustain them, they adapted and became quasi-permanent residents. But now, the separation of two realities on earth—shadow and light—that will eventually split apart is creating much of the energy from which travelers currently feed. So polarized are these realities that belief systems, hardening like armor, are at once capable of keeping out anything that might change them but also of trapping in hope and the potential for expansion. Travelers become caught in our benevolent universe, where they do not belong for they have a dark, malevolent energy with intent to harm. They exist on a thin band of energy that floats just above the third dimension, so they cannot be seen with the human eye. Certain sensitive individuals, however, can soften their vision enough to see traces of them, while others can smell them or feel them hanging around.

Travelers are conscious, but their conscious activity is restricted to finding energy patterns to feed from, recognizing or encouraging such patterns in their human victims, then trapping those individuals in the patterns until their life forces are exhausted. They search especially for humans who have already locked themselves into addictive emotional patterns and thus surrendered their choice. Those at risk on earth include not only depressed individuals and addicts but others such as politicians who refuse to consider anything other than their current beliefs, serial killers, and people who lack control over their lives. The travelers convince their victims to believe that hopeless servitude to their disempowering emotional pattern is inevitable, subsequently ensnaring their victims in energetic tentacles until there is nothing left to feed from. It is a weak sense of self that makes people vulnerable to them. If a traveler exploits a person's vulnerability as it attempts to attach, the individual will feel a revolting energy as their life force is being taken away. Although an unpleasant experience, it is part of a natural cycle of energy that provides a service, like the service provided by a pride of lions taking out sick and injured wildebeests from a herd. Exploiting a person's vulnerability in this way cannot be judged right or wrong, or good or bad; rather, it is to be seen as a means of reformulating the energy of those who cannot sustain a coherent sense of self.

Travelers are not allowed in this dimension, although some of their former victims are here. I asked my teacher why the travelers are excluded from such an open dimension. After all, here we understand that even something "bad" has purpose.

He said: "They are unable to travel here because they cannot locate the frequency of this dimension. Just as you will never have access to certain spaces because they are incompatible with your vibratory field, the same is true of these parasites; they restrict themselves to a level where they can access auric energy fields generated by the living matter from which they feed. When individuals cross over, their auric field changes its energy pattern in such a way that the travelers cannot follow it to this place."

On earth, as individuals change their emotional patterns, their auric field shifts as well, so they are able to provide their own protection as long as they haven't surrendered their personality to addiction or depression. Granted, there is no perfect solution if an individual is hopelessly addicted or depressed, but I am always looking at how humans can walk on earth the way we walk in this dimension.

While on earth there are travelers and others parasites who take from their hosts and give nothing in return, here there are symbiots, described in *My Life after Life*, who add to the experience of the host in exchange for sharing space with them. For example, Wyrme always has to be connected but in exchange provides communication and companionship.

Curious to understand more about the powers of travelers, I asked my teacher, "Has anyone here ever been overpowered by a traveler on earth and then escaped the influence as they left their body?"

He said, "Many individuals in this dimension have had that experience. You have already met some, although you would never suspect that."

I took a moment to figure out who these people might be. An obvious possibility was the homeless woman Sally. Even though she had a strong sense of self, her outside experiences would have kept her in the path of these beings who might have overpowered her as she passed, so I asked my teacher if I was correct.

He answered: "She had such a sense of presence that it allowed her to exist in those circumstances without being taken over or destroyed. She also had an ability to see light and dark and thereby avoided having one of these beings attach to her. Actually, the person you have met who did have one attached was Charles Miller. While he was driven by circumstances to get up and work, he experienced profound depression. It is easy to understand how alcoholics might have their life forces sucked away by one of these parasitic travelers, but it happened to Charles Miller because of his pattern of working on a ship. The fact that he could not change his beliefs, gave up his wife and children, could not see any other path, and ultimately had some satisfaction when death finally took him are clues he had been overpowered. But if you had met him on earth you would not have known he was suffering from this, other than noticing the detachment created by his depression."

I told my teacher, "It is surprising for me to hear this because I liked Charles Miller."

"You don't dislike someone because of such experiences," he answered, laughing. "With a certain understanding of what an energy field should look like, one can see these travelers. Not every depressed, alcoholic, or psychotic human being has been overpowered by one. Actually it is a rare occurrence on earth."

Realizing I had known only a few people who were troubled, withdrawn, or struggled with their life force, I summoned the courage to ask, "Did my mother have one of these travelers?"

My teacher took a deep breath and answered, "No, because even in her deepest depression and in how she dealt with patterns, she never gave up on her family. She never gave up on you."

I was relieved to hear this because I didn't want her or anyone else I know to lack choice and the ability to change their beliefs.

"Once a traveler is connected, it is very difficult to change a belief system without help. Travelers want the individual to stay exactly the same so they can create experiences that will allow them to feed more efficiently. To a traveler, a human victim is just another meal, a moment in their very long-lived lives. Unfortunately there are some individuals who seek out travelers, thinking such an experience will be empowering," my teacher added.

Giving up your life to be a meal for one of these beings seemed incomprehensible to me. Yet I knew there are some who assist an individual under such an attack, just like wildebeest in a herd will come to rescue a member under siege, so having one of these beings attach doesn't mean the individual is automatically lost. But it is necessary to at least have awareness—without superstition or fear—that there is something potentially ominous in one's environment.

My teacher said, "The unseen energy fields of the human body are just as juicy as the body's blood supply, and just as available to nourish an energetic parasite as blood would nourish a tick. Teachers and healers with more advanced understandings of how energy fields relate to the physical body are available to help heal people on earth with this problem, sometimes in addition to methods of traditional medicine."

Although there is much fear and superstition about being possessed, overpowered, or attached to by an unseen entity, especially among those who adhere to the great religious belief systems, rarely is it understood that individuals can find assistance or even strengthen their own energy fields and heal themselves. People should not worry that a bout of depression is anything more than a bout of depression. But when individuals start to identify with their illness, claim they want to get better but cannot, or become detached from life, unable to take advantage of opportunities, it is time to consider that they may have been overpowered by a traveler. Even then, individuals still have some control but cannot recognize their options.

While I do not want to create fear by describing these beings and circumstances, it is important to reveal how people can lose personal freedom.

Editor's note: We have a responsibility to stay balanced. Becoming fanatic or obsessed opens the door to a world of shadows, although even going to the edge doesn't mean something bad will necessarily happen to us. Above all, it is essential to honor our free will and consequent ability to make choices, never surrendering it to any outside influence, authority, or entity. This is truly a matter of "Give me liberty or give me death." We need to see that we are extremely powerful in ways we do not understand and to claim the power of the heart and mind working together.

I was glad to receive reassurance from Galen that his mother had not been overpowered by a traveler. I never stopped loving Galen's mother, even though I spent many years processing the animosity my personality had toward her. It wasn't that I didn't love her but that I didn't know *how* to love her. It has taken me a long time to release the shame and failure associated with this.

Ultimately, we have to understand that there is wisdom in the path an individual follows, whether or not that path looks helpful. Everyone bonds to the patterns and beliefs of the culture into which they are born. The soul then needs certain experiences to change and evolve so everything is in perfect alignment.

*Thomas Paine
(1737–1809)*

CHAPTER 10

Daniel

WAKING UP EVERY MORNING IN MY BED and experiencing the joy of seeing familiar objects sacredly placed where I wanted them sparks my energy for the coming day. On earth I didn't pay much attention to where I placed things, but here my room is very organized. I take pleasure in putting objects in certain places, almost as if I am performing a ritual. Then I walk out my door in anticipation of an interesting day of learning.

On one particular day when I was joyfully anticipating absorbing knowledge, I felt a strong pull to a classroom where there were about ten students. Instead of the usual white walls and green chalkboards, the walls were a beautiful sky-blue color, and the chairs and tables were brightly colored in rainbow hues. The teacher was someone I had worked with before, a scholarly appearing gentleman, and the lecture of the day was about energetic manners—that is, what to do when we meet someone's energy before meeting the person physically. The topic was only pertinent for returning to earth and not for life in this dimension, where there is no potential for conflict or misunderstanding. I looked around to see if any of my classmates was preparing to return to earth, as I have learned to recognize a blue glow outline of such people, but saw none in attendance.

However, I noticed a young man sitting next to me. He was about six feet four with sandy blond hair and a handsome boyish face. He had a collegiate appearance, as if he had just stepped out of catalog featuring the latest pullovers and shirts. I wanted to meet this man, who appeared to be about my age, but he was so focused on the teacher that I couldn't get his attention, even though I tried by clearing my throat and then dropping my pencil on my desk. When the class ended, I caught up with him as he was leaving and said, "Hello, my name is Galen. I have not seen you around before. How are you?"

He introduced himself as Daniel, and as we walked by a tree he pointed toward it and asked, "Would you like to sit here with me?"

"Of course," I said. I would have hung from a branch if it allowed me to get to know this man, for he had a sparkly quality, making him look like a magical creature or someone who had been blessed by fairies. He smiled and moved his body with such perfection it seemed choreographed. I have often pushed myself to meet people so I could learn about them, but never before had I come across someone quite as special.

"How did you get here?" Daniel asked politely.

I told Daniel about my father and mother, my friends at school, how I loved dogs, and how most of my peers didn't have the freedoms that I enjoyed. I told him how fortunate I had been in my life and how I had always known kindness. Finally, I told him about the day I left, being on the tracks when the train came, and the choice I was given to remain or come here.

Daniel was quiet for a moment, reflecting on my story, and then replied: "My life was very different. I didn't look anything like I do now. I was perfectly comfortable with how I looked, but for some reason when I came here this is the appearance I had. I was born with complications from Down's syndrome and with a cleft palate that required several surgeries. My thirteen years were spent homebound, but I learned to do tasks around the house and had parents who loved me dearly and made me feel safe. I also had an older sister named Sharon, whom I loved because she played with me every day as if I were her favorite doll, even once she started going to school.

"After several years I noticed my father wasn't around as much anymore. I would often ask if he was at work and always be told that he was. Only later did I learn that my mother and father had divorced.

"My childhood was very happy, but as I got older there were more and more complications with my body. One day I felt very hot and sick. I was rushed away and remember seeing nurses with their pretty scrubs and stethoscopes. The next thing I knew I was here, being greeted by others. When I asked why my body was so different, I was told this was how my family always saw me—as a perfect and beautiful boy. I know I can create my old form if I want to, but this body reminds me of the love my family has for me and the fact that I was not a burden to them. Even better, I get to go to school! I have a choice now, and I feel very blessed by that."

Daniel and I have been friends for a while now. He is kind, aware, and always radiant. He often talks about returning to earth to be a teacher so he can be connected to school there as well. Although I occasionally remind him that some students don't actually like being at school, I cannot convince him that everyone who goes to school on earth isn't fascinated with it. I am very appreciative of the chance to know him now, as he has such a good attitude about learning and taking advantage of opportunities here.

Whereas many individuals carry their own beliefs into this dimension, Daniel carried with him the beliefs of his family, which gave him a particular image to use here. His situation illustrates the fact that to the soul there is no such thing as disability.

Editor's note: The courage and strength of severely disabled children to stay in their bodies, often fighting for survival, is astonishing. Although some people feel it would be better for these children never to have been born, I disagree since, despite their disabilities, they are able to learn a great deal from their experiences.

A pediatric professor at the first medical school I attended became incensed with me for not counseling prospective parents to get an abortion when they learned they would have a child with Down's syndrome. Instead, I gave a balanced prognosis of what might await such a child, including best- and worst-case scenarios. I knew that some children with Down's syndrome are reasonably high functioning despite their disabilities, and in fact I had heard of a physician who found out he had trisomy 21, the genetic defect responsible for Down's syndrome, but he did not manifest the syndrome, indicating that genetics do not determine everything.[1] I was convinced that the intention of the soul plays an important role as well.

On the other hand, during my residency at UCLA, I sat in while pediatric intensivists tried to tell a Nigerian father that it was in the best interest of his child born with Down's syndrome to continually resuscitate him. This child was severely compromised and would frequently go into cardiac arrest. The father pleaded with the attending physicians to let his child expire, saying that he was hoping to return to Nigeria, where there were no facilities to care for such a severely ill child and he would be allowed to pass. But the physicians would not listen, and continued to do everything possible to keep the child alive until eventually he inevitably died, to the relief of his family. In nature, this child would not have survived, suggesting that just because one *can* save a life does not necessarily

---

[1] According to the new discipline of epigenetics, which addresses the effect environmental factors have on the expression of genes, trisomy 21 would not come to expression if the relevant genes on the redundant chromosome were silenced, which could be accomplished by methylation. This outcome is not known to happen in trisomy 21, but that does not mean it can't happen.

mean one should relentlessly attempt to do so. In this case, repeatedly resuscitating the child, which did not save his life in the long run, was more about winning than seeing wholeness.

Whether to abort a fetus with the genetic defect responsible for Down's syndrome or use extraordinary measures to save one already born should be the choice of the family, not the physician. Many such children come into families to heal some aspect of the family dynamic, resulting in changes such as increased compassion or awareness. Daniel's presence in his family no doubt helped them learn to see past illusions—such as mistaking the body we occupy for the person we are—as they grew in compassion. I am sure his family would agree that his presence was a blessing in their lives. For other families, a child so affected could challenge the shadow side of the psyche and fears of imperfection. Human history is full of examples of scapegoating the differently abled—or even those with unusual beauty or skill—by blaming them for a village curse or whatever fit the politics of the times. Many children who experience such prejudice awaken within their families a heightened awareness of the need to process the pain and anger of limitation not only on a personal level but on a cultural one as well.

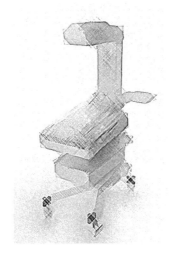

CHAPTER 11

Barbara

MANY INDIVIDUALS HERE HAVE the very human need to contact loved ones left behind, to assure them that they are not in a place of suffering. They try in different ways to communicate and often say it can be frustrating to establish a connection. Given these realities, I feel very fortunate to be able to communicate with my father.

A woman here named Barbara Williams has told me about how, particularly in the beginning, she desperately tried to talk to her family. Barbara said she crossed over in 1953 at age forty-one, after dying quickly and unexpectedly of a massive heart attack, with no history of heart disease. This happened during a large family picnic attended by both young and old, which complicated the potential for communication thereafter since some of them had been traumatized while witnessing the horrific scene as her body went through its death throes. On seeing a healthy woman expire so quickly, they experienced grief and fear of their own mortality.

For Barbara, the event was far less traumatic than for her relatives. She felt a strong punch in her chest, as if someone had hit her, and with that she was instantly out of her body. Since then, she had done her best to communicate with her children and mother, but there were obstacles.

Several methods exist for initiating contact between someone at my dimensional station and someone on earth, although none is effective if the person on earth is closed down in fear or grief. One way to open such communication is for the person on earth to think about the individual on the other side. Doing this will actually form a link to them and open a communication channel to a greater or lesser degree. Although the human on the earth plane may believe they are just thinking about a memory of the person, contact is actually made with the individual in this dimension. In the other direction, the most efficient means of establishing communication with someone on earth is in the dream state, because those on earth are most open while sleeping.

Barbara did eventually contact family members on earth during their dreams, yet the recipients on earth had been so traumatized by seeing her pass in such a dramatic manner that her appearance in dreams frightened them. She would come to them with loving messages, but they would be perceived as ominous, giving her family members a sense of being haunted. For people experiencing grief, fear, or pain it might seem a cruel irony that the very moment when messages from departed loved ones are desired is when they are the most difficult to obtain. Barbara is still trying to get the message to her family that she was immediately released from her body, is now free, and that she loves them and has no intention of disrupting their lives. In the years since her death, some of her family members who attended the picnic have come over to our dimension and she was there to greet them.

I would like everyone to know that those who expire on earth are not "lost" to their loved ones there and that communication is indeed possible. I advise people on earth to do their best to be open to those who pass, since soul and spirit agreements that forge connections do not end just because one party leaves the earth plane. It is human nature for those of us on the other side to desire to reach back to people on earth, and we can feel frustrated by not receiving a response. It is also important for people on earth to realize that the communication established may not resemble the kind I have with my father, in which I dictate long paragraphs and we exchange feelings and memories of familiar songs and other experiences. Even if what I say seems matter-of-fact, there exists between us a constant heart connection, the kind one feels when gathering up a loved one's things to recycle out into the world.

Regardless of the method used to establish communication, clarity of mind is essential to its success. For example, to be of clear mind people for whom a family member went missing must get past the fear of finding out their loved one may have passed or that they are living somewhere else on earth and no longer care about their family. While such clarity can't be programmed, the ability to welcome communication can be developed using some techniques. The first step is for individuals to set an intention to be open to a loved one. The next step is to surrender to a state of attentive allowance, remaining observant and open.

It is also possible to establish communication with individuals who have lived and died alone and who have no one on earth with whom they'd like to connect. While some have chosen their isolation, others have simply been forgotten. Such individuals are in need of acknowledgment; and fortunately, people on earth have the ability, during quiet reflection, to make contact with them and thus help them. This kind of work is not for everyone, but there are many intuitive people on earth who can be a bridge to those who have been forgotten.

Then, too, some cultures have a lovely practice of honoring ancestors without knowing their specific identities. In doing this, individuals not only send feelings of gratitude to the ancestors but also establish a loving connection with them that simultaneously supports the living. People can better understand this, perhaps, if in honoring the Tomb of the Unknown Soldier they would send a telepathic message to all individuals who died unknown, telling them they are not forgotten and that their earth life had value. In all likelihood such people, even if they heard no words from the soldiers' spirits, would still feel they have made a connection in their hearts.

Of course, the deceased who have passed on alone are not stuck waiting for someone to acknowledge them, as eventually everyone moves forward on their path. But there are still plenty who could benefit from some thoughtful appreciation, just as a lonely solder might appreciate a box of cookies sent by a stranger from home. Conveying appreciation for those who have passed is fundamentally an act of respect. As the cycles move forward, obstacles to communication from earth to this dimension will not be as problematic as they are now; until then, every effort made on earth to communicate to this dimension, even sending anonymous greetings to unknown individuals, hastens the day when that will be so.

While there is wisdom in not having unfettered communication between our dimensions, there should be no concern that generic messages of appreciation will fall into the wrong hands. Those who have used the learning opportunities on earth disrespectfully move through well-supervised processes of energetic realignment and are no less worthy of blessing than anyone else. There is no punishment here. Such individuals are instead held back, having to relearn and re-earn the privilege to manifest as humans, though still they are human.

Remember, crossing to this dimension does not automatically make individuals more insightful. Therefore, communication conveying anything beyond a loving heart connection is best reserved for unusual circumstances. In fact, all such communication requires discernment. Even the most well-intentioned efforts at interdimensional communication are subject to filters employed by the human brain, especially beliefs, wishes, hopes, and fears.

Much about the availability of life and energy is not understood. Life is everywhere, and it will use anything at hand to manifest. Earth scientists believe the right conditions must exist for there to be life, but this is actually backwards, for life is omnipresent in every dimension. The conditions required to have organic carbon-based life are created by the life force that was always there, and if carbon isn't available life will pick something else at a suitable level and frequency. So whether it is a human, a bird, a tree, or a whale, the life you see animating these carbon-based manifestations is the tip of a cosmic iceberg in which all life is connected.

When the physical body dies, an individual's consciousness, which is an integral part of the life force, shifts into another realm that life has created, hence the continuum principle. Life does not destroy itself just because the carbon-based shell it was using can no longer hold its form in a functional manner. Because there is no separation, when you look into the eyes of another, you are truly looking into your own eyes. What's more, even when those eyes are no longer in front of you or were never carbon based in your dimension in the first place, you can send love and connectedness to anybody anywhere.

༄ ༄ ༄

Editor's note: Here Galen clearly describes the universal laws under which we operate. There is an all-pervasive life force from which we all come and to which we are all connected, as well as an underlying continuum of consciousness. Whether we call this wholeness God or nature or the Great I is secondary to glimpsing the macrocosm and understanding how we fit into it.

If we can accept Galen's words as truth, then it is indeed an act of compassion to attempt to contact a departed loved one from our hearts to provide them with peace and relieve them of the frustration they may feel while sending messages to us here on earth. It might mean everything to a recently passed loved one if we were to say something like, "I can't see you with my eyes or touch you with my flesh, but from my heart to your heart I send a loving blessing of gratitude and appreciation until the day we can once again hold each other in the same space and time. You will never be forgotten—love is forever."

CHAPTER 12

Beth

AT MY DIMENSIONAL STATION, there are no holidays to celebrate. But it is as if we celebrate here every day. Also, since we can use our imagination to alter the appearance of our environment, if I want to duplicate Halloween or Christmas I do so. However, even now, after having a better feel for how things work here, I still miss the holidays on earth. In spite of all the connectedness that exists at this dimensional station, others here also share sentimental feelings about earth holidays. There is a general human desire for anticipating and planning specific occasions just to experience the vibrations of gatherings where people are in sync. The feeling of unity at those moments is a break from the polarity that exists the rest of the time on earth. Imagine how incredible it would be if humanity could generate that same unity to accomplish something like cleaning up an ocean!

One reason I am drawn to the new arrivals from earth is that I miss not only earth celebrations but earth energy in general. When I meet individuals from earth who have been here for a long time, their vibration is different from my own. But when I meet those who have been here for only a short time, there is a very human energy about them. Just as I can see the blue glow around individuals about to return to earth, when someone is about to transition to this dimension I can sense it. The air crackles with a static charge akin to an approaching lightning storm, and there is a familiar scent of humans on earth, as if they have just walked through a certain perfume. When I start missing my family, it is with these new arrivals that I find a sense of connectedness. To experience such connectedness, I have begun to pay more attention when I see new individuals coming in with teachers, relatives, or beings reflecting their belief systems, to assist in their integration. Instead of watching from afar, I move in closer to the paths on which they arrive. Even though teachers introduce themselves to the newly arrived and explain their situations, I can sometimes sense their fear and loss, as well as their surprise. The faces of some look as though they do not understand what has just happened; since we all have respect for their state of confusion, we do not approach them immediately. I make an effort to look carefully into their faces and just smile a greeting.

One day a certain woman being escorted in by two teachers caught my attention. She appeared to be in her early forties, was wearing business clothes—a blazer and skirt with high heels—and looked panic-stricken. Soon she started to sob, begging to be taken back. Her teachers, one on each side of her, surrounded her with love and spoke to her for some time, but she kept shaking her head no. To my surprise, they took her back out through the doorway, something I hadn't realized was possible. I stood there for what felt like about fifteen minutes of earth time because I knew they eventually had to return since this was not the path back to earth life. After a while they did return, and this time the woman was escorted by what looked like a little girl; she had her hand on the little girl's shoulder and would occasionally touch the child's head. But this little girl was more a hologram than a human. Generally, newcomers look around as if they are checking out a new house they are about to move into but the woman was gazing about with very wide eyes, having no idea what was happening to her. The girl image, however, seemed to help her. I had never seen someone have such a difficult time on arrival, and I was very interested in learning more about her.

Later, I met up with her and found her calm and collected despite the fact that the little girl image was nowhere to be seen. The woman introduced herself as Beth Moran, and I said, "I saw you when you came in, and you looked very afraid."

"I was terrified. I thought I was dreaming but couldn't wake up. People were talking to me, and I had no idea who they were or why I was here. I understand now that I am dead and this is my next experience," Beth replied.

I asked, "Do you want to talk about what happened?"

"I don't know what happened. I was at work, with a meeting scheduled, and all I remember was a sort of pop in the middle of my head. I couldn't see anything and felt a pulsing. When my eyes could focus again, I saw two strangers standing in front of me. I thought maybe aliens had abducted me," she answered, laughing.

I told her about my own experiences and what I have come to understand. As our conversation continued, it became clear that on earth she had no belief in an afterlife, which explains some of the confusion she experienced upon arrival.

Because she didn't believe in an afterlife, every morning upon waking she knew she had to make each moment count. But she focused so much on controlling everything to get ahead that she had little presence of mind in her earth life, so naturally she had just as little when she passed.

"I don't know what was driving me. It seems that if you think you have only one life you would slow down and enjoy each moment. But instead, I drove myself hard. When I crossed over, I thought the two teachers helping me were my coworkers taking me to my office to lie down. But I ended up in this land with green grass, and it freaked me out," she said.

"I was watching how they took you back—what did they do?" I asked, with curiosity.

"When we went back, they showed me my last moments. And while watching the process my body had gone through, I understood more," she answered.

"I saw you walking back with a young child. Was that your daughter?" I asked.

"No. I planned to have children, but it never seemed like the time was right for me to have them."

She continued, saying, "The teachers told me they were giving me something very important that I had lost. When I looked at the little girl's face, I sensed that she belonged to me and I wanted to keep her close. She helped calm me down by escorting me into heaven.

"Eventually I realized that the little girl was me. Somehow that imaginative child who was happy believing in fairies had separated from me at a certain point in my life, and she was given back to me when I arrived here. As soon as I realized this, she disappeared. I haven't really been frightened since. I still don't know if I believe in heaven or hell, but what I do believe is that I am right here in this moment and this is the path I walk right now. Here I am going to make every moment count. I have no idea what comes after this. They tell me I have a choice about going back to earth or staying. They tell me I can do anything I want. But for today I am fine sitting right here talking to you and not feeling I have to push myself to do something," she said.

She had clearly learned something very important on a spirit and soul level about being in the moment. Beth had never experienced enjoyment except when she had been a child, represented by the little girl. Her teachers had located that forgotten part of herself, the imaginative little child, and knew it could help her find peace in her new dimension. The teachers do not force individuals into this dimension, but find ways to help them step into this space, because the consciousness must open up to be at this dimensional station.

I long to have such human connections with those who have recently arrived, and I wonder if I could work as one of these helpers for a while. There was a time when I wanted to rush back to earth because I thought that was the only way I could feel human connections again. But I am beginning to understand that the bridge to earth provided by conversations with individuals who have recently arrived from there are giving me a chance to become integrated in this dimension by helping others on a regular basis. My interests may change, of course, because I am always learning; and instead of deciding what I need to do, I must remain constantly open to possibilities. Fortunately the push and pull of experiences present on earth does not exist because polarity is not operational here.

෨ ෨ ෨

Editor's note: I wondered why Beth was plucked out of her earth life in the prime of her adulthood in that particular way. When I asked Galen and his teachers, I was told it wasn't about her lifestyle or lack of imagination because she obviously had imagination, although it had been suppressed. Rather, she had been born with a congenital weakness in the wall of a blood vessel in her brain, a condition that can lead to sudden death without warning. She certainly wasn't prepared to leave at that moment, but it was the one chosen by her physical body. One might argue that this moment of death had been predetermined at the time of her birth, but behind what often appears as fate are choices that were made. When individuals such as Beth do not believe there is something beyond the physical body because of a brain aneurysm or other cause, they might have little choice but to think they have lost touch with reality. However, lack of belief in an afterlife did not stop Beth from eventually arriving at Galen's dimensional station; her soul vibration and spiritual maturity brought her there, not her belief system.

Others with less spiritual maturity but with the same belief system might find themselves in a state of limbo until it slowly sinks in that they are prisoners of their own lack of imagination. For example, when my uncle, who did not believe in an afterlife, passed way twenty-five years ago, I found him in a hospital bed on the other side. His persona had assumed that since he was still conscious he must be in the same situation he had been in before leaving earth, hence the hospital bed. I noticed he was moving the side of his body that had been affected by a stroke and wondered how long it would take him to figure that out. At the time, I didn't think it was my role to point this out to him, as I was just there to say hello.

The purpose of being in a body on earth is not to prepare for the inevitable departure from that body but to be present enough to experience it in the moment. The fact that conditions in Galen's realm support constant openness to new possibilities is probably why he feels every day there is like a holiday, indicating he is present to experience in his new dimension, and thus on his path.

There is great wisdom in Beth's statement about being "right here in this moment." Unaware that many Buddhist masters strive to find that moment of now, she had discovered something profound without understanding how she had arrived at it. She will undoubtedly take that understanding into her next experience, awakening a new perspective. That might seem like small consolation, but ultimately things are the way they are and individuals must strive to have an open heart and move on. The trust implicit in such openhanded living is that it will result in the best for all. In the big picture, Beth's passing is a tragedy only to those left behind who have to pick up the pieces and face doubts about life's meaning. The continuum of consciousness brings little solace to those who lack access to the larger picture.

I am told that the soul is neutral, without an agenda, and evolves as everything else in the universe evolves, though if it did have an agenda, I suppose things would be more understandable to humans.

CHAPTER 13

Jaloo

T̲h̲e̲ ̲e̲x̲p̲e̲r̲i̲e̲n̲c̲e̲s̲ ̲h̲e̲r̲e̲ ̲o̲f̲t̲e̲n̲ ̲r̲e̲f̲l̲e̲c̲t̲ the experiences people had before they arrived, regardless of where they were previously, because individuals usually perceive what they believe. People from earth generally wouldn't see a non-earthling if such a being were standing in front of them. And this place looks to individuals just like they thought heaven and its inhabitants would look. The outdoor environment reflects the collective agreement of what everyone here would like to see. That doesn't mean everything is homogeneous, for sometimes I will come across a very unusual tree or plant, and the sky isn't always blue. Both in my local "town" and also beyond it there is great diversity and always something in the environment that arouses one's curiosity and desire to learn. I believed there was life on other planets and dimensions, so that is reflected in the diversity of my experiences in my realm. Conversely, Beth didn't believe in an afterlife, so she didn't perceive this dimension to be heaven until she had managed to expand her perspective.

What causes individuals to be put here or there is the potential they have to be expansive by altering their perspective. Those around me tend to be expansive and self-observing, allowing them to constantly learn and progress.

For individuals from earth, having a silver cup containing the sum total of our earthly experiences, which we can access and build on, assists this development. But as I have learned, individuals from other systems retain and access past experiences in a quite different manner. One day, I was sauntering along with my hands in my pants pockets when I noticed people gathering in small groups and talking to one another. In the distance I could see a boy of about eight darting around people and foliage. I had never seen this boy before. He had no hair, wore robes, and had a half-filled sack flung over his shoulder, making me think he was a young monk; but he had very light-colored skin, so I knew he wasn't Asian. His erratic movements made him look like the comic superhero The Flash, but they were also keeping him from advancing toward his goal and eventually caused him to stumble and almost fall. Although he caught himself, the contents of his sack fell to the ground, at which point he threw his hands up in frustration and dropped to his knees to pick up about twenty luminescent orbs the size of tennis balls, which were pearl-white with a slight hint of blue and glowed from their centers.

I picked up my pace, knowing I could now catch up with the boy. When I got close enough to assist him in picking up the orbs, I reached down, saying, "Hello, my name is Galen. Let me help you."

With the strength of a grown man, he grabbed my wrist and said, "Don't touch them!"

His voice, while firm, had a wonderful baritone resonance, and now I could see he was not an eight-year-old boy.

My gaze turned to his sack, which was ornate, with intricately embroidered symbols. "That sack is exquisite," I said.

"Thank you. My grandmother made it for me," he answered.

"Are you in a hurry? Do you have a moment to talk?" I asked him.

"Oh yes, I have plenty of time to talk. Today I am just wandering without a particular destination," he replied.

We sat under a tree to have a relaxing conversation. I told him about myself and my family, then he introduced himself as Jaloo and asked me where I was from.

"I'm from Santa Fe, New Mexico," I replied.

"No, no, where are you from?" he asked emphatically.

"I'm from earth," I answered, suddenly realizing that he must be from another planet. He looked human except for being short and having translucent pink skin with a slight glow, as well as large soft eyes with irises reflecting a fine fluted pattern that was repeated on a smaller scale at the pupil.

"Ah yes, there are many of you here," he answered.

"Where are you from?" I asked with curiosity.

"My planet is called Kreh and is in the Andromeda Galaxy," he replied.

I studied his robes, enjoying their unusual combination of colors—red paired with green, and purple with orange. The cloth was finely embroidered with symbols. Otherwise similar to monks' robes, it had a slightly raised mandarin collar, a jacket fastened in the front, and loose-fitted pants with straight legs.

"Your clothes are very finely made. What are all those symbols?" I asked.

"They are prayers my grandmother placed on them about my journey here. My family and society are matriarchal. Mothers and grandmothers are like royalty, deciding how everything is to be in our society. When I became ill, my grandmother made the clothes so I could wear my story while passing out of my body," he confided.

"I wondered if you had such an experience, because you seem full of life," I commented. "Yes, I died of an illness at a young age," he replied.

"What are those orbs that spilled out of your sack?" I asked.

"You don't have these?" Jaloo asked with a quizzical expression on his face.

"No, I don't have orbs," I answered.

Jaloo explained, "Each orb is a recording of one of my life cycles, representing experiences that I can connect to as part of my journey."

"When I came here, I was given a little silver cup that contained my experiences," I said.

"Yes, I have one of those as well," he replied, pulling it out from under his robes.

"Then I don't understand why you also have orbs. Are those orbs for each year?" I said.

"No, our life cycles are not measured in years, months, or days, but in experiences. The orbs are like the growth rings of a tree or a crystal that grows new layers. In my world, whenever we complete a cycle of understanding, it is like our life begins anew. We live a very long time, with a continuum between the cycles we move through. The experiences of each cycle are contained in an orb, which we keep with us as we advance to the next life cycle. We do eventually die, be it from an accident or an illness, though it is very rare for us to die of old age," he explained.

"Many who leave their body and travel to another dimension will have five sacks of orbs with them. I only have one half of one sack, so as you can see I had a short life. I didn't want you to touch them because the energy and experiences they contain would be dispersed, but you can look at them," he explained.

Jaloo held an orb up for me to see, and I felt as if I were being drawn into it by some magnetic attraction. In the orb I saw a bird in flight, moving with the same rhythm that Jaloo had when walking. I thought perhaps all beings on Kreh moved that way.

"I am seeing what looks like a bird. Was that your pet?" I asked.

"No, that's me. In my past experience, I wanted to know what it felt like to live in that being so I transformed my energy. Where I come from individuals have the ability to merge with or create any form they wish."

"Do you mean the same as it is here?" I asked.

"Yes, it is the same as it is here in the sense that when you are able to visualize something, you can experience it. But on Kreh we are able to maintain a form until we feel the experience is complete, at which time it is put into an orb. When I depart from here to go back to Kreh, I will leave these orbs behind, and they will become part of this dimension, as I won't return to Kreh with memories but will have completely new experiences."

Humans record their experiences on shiny flat disks called DVDs. It's not the same thing, by any means, but DVDs might seem almost as strange to outsiders, I thought to myself. "In my experience the soul is a container, and I continue to learn from that process," I said aloud.

"We have such a process as well. But I will go back with no memory of what happened before and will depend on my family to recognize me as I come in. So just before I go I will send them dreams with forms, and they will begin to look for me," he added.

"That is a great idea, perhaps something I should try with my family," I replied, and we laughed together.

I learned all I could about Krehin society. People there are evolving through the chakra system and are now working on the high chakras. While humans on earth are also using the chakra system on their evolutionary path, they are just beginning to explore the heart chakra, above which lies the throat chakra, the mid-brow chakra of the third eye, the crown chakra, and finally the high chakras, an upside-down reflection of the known chakra system.

The level where I currently am is part of the fifth dimension, while Kreh is between the third and fourth dimensions. This explains the sense of expansion and profundity reflected in Jaloo's eyes in comparison with human eyes, which indicates higher consciousness—much like what I saw in Andy's eyes. When I decide to come back to earth, I will greatly miss the inspiration and incredible energy to be derived from the eyes of beings who experience alternate dimensions.

Humanity on earth is currently undergoing a tremendous experience evolving into the heart chakra, but more generations will need to be born into this before it stabilizes, although its influence on society is already apparent. One hundred years from now most humans will still not be born with their heart chakras open, but enough will have them open to take humanity into the next phase of its evolution. A thousand years from now, humanity will be a little closer to how individuals are on Kreh, though not with the same beliefs or the practice of encasing experiences in glowing orbs. It may take well over ten thousand years for humankind to be dimensionally where the Krehins are now. Evolution is a slow process that comes from within, not one imposed from the outside, although external events can have an influence.

Krehins are still influenced by polarity and have humanoid bodies common to systems in which polarity operates, but they are working with a higher octave of polarity—the experiential rather than choice through cause and effect, the aspect that takes place on earth. Many planets operate at the dimensional level that Kreh occupies and many other planets operate at a lower octave of the third dimension than what earth utilizes.

Another notable difference between the earth and Kreh is that people returning to earth do not incarnate with a slate clean to the same extent as those returning to Kreh. Individual humans bring in many talents and memories, including memories of lineage, even if most remain in their subconscious minds. By contrast, it is the family who remembers lineage on Kreh, and individuals are reborn into the same lineage. While Jaloo will not remember his original family when he returns, they will remember him, and he will be welcomed and honored as a returned family member. Physical lineage holds the memory for those on Kreh, while spiritual lineage holds the memory for humans. When a human remembers a past life or a past connection, it is literally being pulled up through the spiritual lineage. Because Kreh memories are held in the physical lineage, there is no need to carry experiences and they are released to universal energy, making those reborn freer to have new experiences.

The death process is also a little different on Kreh. When Jaloo left Kreh, his orbs of memory went with him because they are him. So family members watching the process would have seen his sack of orbs disappear, even though the shell that was his body remained behind, just as physical bodies do on earth. The finely embroidered robe Jaloo wears is a reproduction of the one his grandmother created for him on Kreh, just as my clothes are a reproduction of what I had been wearing on earth.

On various occasions I continued to introduce Jaloo to things I have discovered here in this dimension. At the same time, I learned all I could about life on the planet Kreh, as I find the variations in lifestyles of people from different planets most educational.

୨୭ ୨୭ ୨୭

Editor's note: Evolution is not imposed from outside us but comes from within. Cause and effect influences from the outside did not take dinosaurs to a higher dimension; instead, they just removed the vast majority of these creatures from the planet, birds being the notable exception. On the other hand, as attitudes, beliefs, and emotions shift, they create a different external expression. For instance, when the first fish crawled out of the sea and took a breath, it was not because some external event or power attached lungs or glued on legs; rather, it was a result of crawling out of the sea and taking a breath by choice, which allowed that lineage to spend more time in the shallows and then take short trips out of the water. Such excursions gave this lineage of fish a survival and reproductive advantage because they chose to move in that direction. There are individuals who believe some grand ascension is just around the corner, but when one steps back to look at how nature expresses itself ascension occurs because an evolution is happening within.

I asked Galen about Jaloo's presence at this dimensional station. Was it unusual for Krehins to visit this realm, and if not, why did Galen only encounter this one inhabitant from Kreh? I suspected the answer to my second question was that most Krehins stayed on their planet, because there they lived long lives, barring an occasional accident or illness.

Galen confirmed my guess, adding that Krehins sometimes arrived in his realm between bodies, but the vast majority bypassed the between-life state, preferring to be absorbed and recycled without reviewing memories or processing incomplete experiences. This option suited them well since the high octave of polarity with which they worked, as opposed to beings on earth, did not leave a great deal to be understood as so little was misunderstood.

Curious about Jaloo's age as well, I made some quick calculations. The twenty orbs in his sack only half filled it, so I figured that if each orb correlated with an experience that encompassed a decade or two (translated into linear earth time) Jaloo could have been anywhere between two hundred and four hundred years old. If a full sack contained forty orbs, an individual with five such sacks, the amount Jaloo indicated most Krehins usually leave with, would have at least two thousand years of life-cycle experience in one incarnation, and perhaps twice that many.

CHAPTER 14

All Dogs Go to Heaven (Sort of)

Andy had been my dog here until he left, and in a way he represented several dogs I had known on earth, including a black Lab named Doc that I was helping to train for the Assistance Dogs of the West. During the time Andy was with me, I would see other individuals with their pets—not only dogs but also cats, birds, and horses. And while no doubt some of them had been created just to give a sense of comfort to individuals who had passed, others were certainly like Andy—teachers in the form of pets.

I have since learned to distinguish between these types of animals. When an animal is a manifestation of a teacher, it has the look of higher consciousness in its eyes. Gazing into Andy's eyes, it was easy to tell there was a higher being inhabiting his form. An animal created out of the imagination of another individual emits a high hum, a vibration that, while not audible, gives you the sense that you are looking at a kind of energy with no life force behind it. The individuals I interact with are *real*, with a life force and memories, rather than just imprints of information in an energy field.

One day I spotted three guys about my age playing Frisbee with their dogs. I sat down on the grass to watch because I love the interaction between dogs and humans. Immediately a white dog with brown patches, which looked like a mix between an English Springer Spaniel and a Pit Bull, came to me panting and wagging his tail. I looked into his eyes thinking I would see the same sort of higher consciousness that had been visible in Andy's eyes; but instead, I realized I was looking into the eyes of a real dog rather than a disguised teacher.

The other two dogs—a black Lab mix and a small terrier—also appeared to be real dogs. I approached their owners and asked, "What are the names of your dogs?" The young men called out the names of their dogs—Butch, Sandy, and Wally.

"Did you meet up with them here?" I asked.

They told me the dogs were waiting for them when they arrived, then one said, "Wally had been my dog when I was a young boy, but was hit by a car and died. I missed him a lot, even though I had a dog after him who was still alive when I passed. One day after arriving here, I was walking along when Wally came over a hill and ran up to me."

I wondered why none of my earth dogs that had passed had met me here and why the Frisbee players' pets were present.

When I later asked my teacher this question, he said, "Certain animals on earth have formed a deep bond with their human's experiences. Because of their awareness, they integrate into this dimension. They don't always stay a long time but long enough to interact with their humans."

"I had a close connection with my dogs, so how come I didn't meet them here?" I asked.

My teacher replied, "There wasn't a need to. You did not have an uncompleted agreement with your dogs like those young men did. Their dogs came to complete a cycle with them."

"Do people's pets come only because of that?" I asked.

"Sometimes they are here to help complete this dimension for humans who have become dependent on them. Humans seek out animal companionship for a sense of completion within themselves. They help humans connect to their instincts and earth nature. In short, so many of the animals you find here are committed to human interaction," he added.

To better understand the role of my dog Andy, who for me had been the sum total of beloved dog, multidimensional being, and teacher, I asked, "Do other animals leave like Andy did—by making a loud pop and disappearing into the air?"

"No. Andy left that way because a portal was open. Most dogs just go back over the hill to reenter bodies elsewhere and continue their own evolution. Because of their work with humans, those returning to earth bring with them a deepening awareness of their spirituality. Animals serve the human experience, for they do not separate instinct and spirit, and they model that space for humans to emulate on a higher level," he answered.

Even in this dimension the connection between dogs, cats, birds, horses, and humans assist processing. Humans help animals evolve and develop awareness of their spirits, and vice versa. But here, unlike on earth, when you miss someone, as I miss Andy, you gain understanding that everything is okay. On an emotional level, the adjustment is quick, without the deep mourning or sense of loss that is customary on earth. Therefore, if an individual having a strong bond with an animal needs to complete a cycle of understanding with this animal, the animal will be here for them when they pass so this can be accomplished.

The universe would not be so beautiful and diverse without the participation of many animals, which, like us, are sentient beings. Some that move through my realm don't look like earth animals. In fact, it is interesting when out walking to come upon a creature and wonder if it is a projection from someone's imagination or if it belongs to a being here. You usually determine whether a creature is real or illusory by sensing its vibration. Unfortunately it is a little more difficult on earth to distinguish between reality and illusion, which is why it is a planet of polarity.

Although the dimension I am in is teeming with life, there is a more harmonic energy here than on earth and therefore no need for animals to feed on one another or for people to fear being killed or injured by one. Here a lion and a deer, a cat and dog, a squirrel and ferret, or a human and a bear can walk together. But dogs still go around lifting their legs because after all, they still have dog minds and energy.

Some levels of this dimension, however, support certain animals more than others. For example, you won't see a polar bear strolling through the park here unless you deliberately create a fake bear through your imagination. But if it is your intention to meet a real polar bear on a glacier or ice floe, you will because they are there, since their memory of familiar spaces keeps them in such environments.

෨෨ ෨෨ ෨෨

Editor's note: Galen's observations about dogs in his dimension reminded me of several experiences I'd had with the passing of dogs. The first was a trip to the veterinary clinic that Galen, his mother, and I took when he was about two years old. Our dog Willie, a German Shepherd and Welsh corgi mix, was very sick, and we all watched as the veterinarian put him down. When we started walking out the door, Galen said, without looking back, "Come on, Willie." Obviously, Galen was too young to understand what had just taken place. To a child of that age, there is no distinction between life and death.

Another experience involving a dog passing made me aware of how we can't know the deeper reasons for the passing of humans and animals. As a teen, I was driving my mom's car to a tennis court at UCLA when I saw an elderly neighbor whose wife had recently passed pull into his driveway and get out of the car. His small white terrier jumped out and bolted across the street, hitting my right front tire. I stopped the car in disbelief, retrieved the lifeless dog, and carried it to the old man, who was understandably angry. I apologized profusely and pointed out that there was nothing I could have done. I felt bad for him, but I was not the one to console him. When, several months later, I heard that the old man himself had passed, I couldn't help but think that I might have contributed to that situation, which made me feel much worse about the dog incident.

When I asked Galen about this episode, I was told that companion animals intimately connected to their owners can often be holding space for them. The little white terrier was doing what it did every day with great exuberance and no conscious intent to commit suicide, but it had belonged to the wife who had passed earlier and, on some level, sensed that the husband would eventually die. Consequently, in a strange way, what happened that day served on many levels. The dog was not going to have a happy home after the man passed, and the old man was relieved of having to take care of the dog as he became ill. In the moment it seemed tragic, frightening, and even confusing, but thanks to Galen's observation, the reasons for the incident were now apparent to me. I could see the balance that took place.

In his posthumously published novel entitled *The Mysterious Stranger,* Mark Twain introduced the concept that intervening in an apparent tragedy often creates another tragedy of greater proportions, and like it or not, tragic circumstances are often the most compassionate options available for reasons we mortals cannot comprehend. Events that don't make sense to us and seem to come out of nowhere often occur to bring balance on levels we cannot fathom with our earthly sensibilities. I had some sense of this when Galen passed, but that did not help me process the incident. I doubt that I would still be here on earth had I not eventually received an expanded understanding of the spiritual events surrounding Galen's accident—for my heart would have soon given out. Understanding how one circumstance affects another and how a tragedy might reflect compassion creates a powerful perspective.

After extensive dialogues with Galen and others, I learned that a dog's experience on earth (there are dogs on other planets) is different from that of a human. Dogs are instinctually connected to the energetic grid of the earth and therefore are the definitive teachers regarding being in an earth body. Humans have removed themselves from this connection through a variety of illusions and beliefs, leading to the agreement we have to consciously—not instinctually—reconnect with the wholeness that is our true reality.

Dogs cycle not only with the earth but also with human experience. The ones that are devoted to human experience, usually the domesticated breeds that have come to interact with and depend on humans, are highly attuned to the experiences around them and many times act as healers for their human companions. Because dogs are instinctually geared toward being members of a pack that they would normally give their love and devotion to, when a human is perceived as part of that pack they will give that person respect and love as a natural extension of themselves.

Another unique aspect of dogs on earth is that while they have a strong instinct to stay alive they have no difficulty letting go. When a dog passes, its experience on the other side can be very quick. Some take short side lives as other animals and then return to the pack more developmentally advanced. Those who are complete with the pack energy may instead choose an experience offering more independence; typically they move toward the energy they feel connected to, and consequently some will choose human experience.

When I asked if a human would ever prefer to move back into animal form, I was told that has apparently occurred but the desire to move into an animal body following the experience of separation is very rare. More often the wish is to evolve forward from the conscious sense of individuation into an experience of conscious wholeness. Having completed such an understanding and achieved wholeness in human form on earth, this ascended soul will expand into another experience while giving parts of itself to every conscious being, including those continuing to evolve toward wholeness on earth so they can directly benefit from this accomplishment as well.

Galen also helped me resolve questions that had been plaguing me for decades about the abuse and neglect of domestic dogs and other animals. How, I wondered, could a loving God allow animals to undergo pain and suffering at the hands of the humans who care for them? Do these creatures have a different experience of mistreatment than humans? What comfort can they find on earth in such circumstances? And why would they choose to reenter life as a domestic animal when they are likely to be subjected to cruelty?

I was informed that Source—in this case, a loving God—is dedicated to serving the highest good for all. In this context the question, then, is not about God taking care of beings who are in need of compassion, but rather how we ourselves take care of those beings, how we create compassion and understanding, and how we provide the care, love, and support of our fellow creatures in keeping with our view of the equality of life. Although animals do not have the illusions common to humans or live in states of separation, they do feel fear and pain, despair and sadness. So it is really up to us all to treat the animals in our lives as expressions of God—to honor and respect them as the teachers and healers that they are. Having lost sight of how and with whom we share our planet is one more symptom of humankind's separation from nature and natural instinct. So for now, animals endure cruelty for the benefit of humans who need to learn that cruelty is not a useful energy.

Nathaniel Stoller, sketched on the USS Kitkun Bay *during World War II.*

CHAPTER 15

Nathaniel

A PERSON I'VE ENCOUNTERED HERE three times who has helped me with my sojourn is my dad's father, Nathaniel. My grandfather is not someone I would normally cross paths with because even though he passed only a decade before me he had already returned his cup to its shelf in the Hall of Cups and expanded onto a different level. He was able to do this because he did not need to hold the form of his last earth incarnation and interact with this dimension the way I do. By contrast, I have chosen to hold this form because I enjoy the creative possibilities afforded me as a result. My grandfather remains connected to this dimension only when there is a special reason, and I became such a reason after I first arrived.

You don't have to have a visible or physical presence to hold space here; you can choose to expand and rest. Those who choose this path often return to their planets as intuitive individuals because of their expanded consciousness. The challenge for them is to remain grounded in their physical bodies while practicing *discernment*—not in the polarized sense of distinguishing between what is right or wrong but by subtly feeling energies guiding them as they progress on their paths. Discernment provides balance and is very much a part of the evolution into the heart chakra.

Although I have had three actual visits with my grandfather, his energy is with me every moment. Each day as I walk through this dimension, my grandfather's vibration recognizes my vibration and he is always available for emotional grounding if I need it. I have not interacted with my grandfather for a while because I have been able to ground myself through long family conversations with my father. My grandfather also benefits from my connection with my father since it provides companionship.

I first met up with my grandfather here when I was drawn to an office building, much as I am drawn to a classroom. I just had a feeling I needed to be in this building. I went up a couple of floors, opened the door to an office, and saw my grandfather—or a representation of him—sitting at a desk. His personality was present enough for him to converse with his grandson in a manner reflecting wisdom and openness.

After he walked around the desk to greet me, we shook hands and embraced. He said jokingly, "Did you come to apply for a job?" Then, in a more serious tone, he added, "I am sorry you are here," meaning he was sorry that my life on earth had ended so soon. We sat on a couch and chatted about my plans until I sensed that he needed to get back to something. So I stood up and said, "Good to see you." We embraced again and I said, "I will see you later," to which he replied, "Any time you wish."

The last two times I saw him he looked like he was busy doing something practical, as if he were engaged in everyday activities. The final time I saw him I had been drawn to a market square where he appeared to be shopping. While we were meeting each other, everything seemed very natural, although at other times I had no awareness of the localities where we met. It was as if they appeared magically for the sole purpose of our encounter.

I did not know that at the time of these conversations with my grandfather he was appearing for my benefit alone. When it becomes time to reincarnate, he will transition to his previously held human form, take on the blue glow associated with this phase of reintegration with the material dimension, have conversations with his teachers, review contracts and agreements, and then return to earth. But in the meantime, to support me he is simply holding space and not going anywhere. It is often those holding formless space who make connections in dreams to family members on earth. Then something about family pulls such individuals out of the atmosphere.

The souls of such individuals participate in these decisions and interact with other souls. When ready, they take on form again here in preparation for moving back into a material body. I find it comforting, as I walk around, to know that there are some here who can come in and connect with others if necessary.

The choice they make to be formless is not because they don't want to participate but simply to have a different experience for a cycle of time. For some, an agreement to have this type of experience may already be in place, dating back to a time before they transitioned out of their earth bodies. Since such individuals are here for a while, even by universal time standards, they may also be waiting for a particular moment to arrive on a specific planet in order to transition back into form during a period of change, as many are doing now on earth.

While my grandfather has apparently chosen to hold space and rest, I have chosen to actively engage in opportunities for manifesting. Remaining in my form gives me possibilities for creative expression. Others, such as Charles Miller, may choose to go to school or have conscious interactions with others and the landscape. Here it is like theater: you can interact with energy in any way you wish. The preferences one has about how to move forward are not so different from those that people make every day on earth about how to participate in life. Because of their state of "beingness" in this realm, those who choose to be formless are likely to become deep thinkers and intuitives when they return to earth, while those opting for form, like Charles Miller, are apt to become manifesters. There is no fixed rule about how individuals spend their next earth incarnations apart from soul agreements.

Editor's note: I had a dream about my father after he passed in 1999, an experience that seems to echo and amplify Galen's. In the dream, I met my father on the other side. I had the strong impression I was walking in the social area of a school building where there were round tables with tablecloths—seemingly a place where tea or coffee was served in an informal manner. I saw him leaning back in a chair, which was slightly pushed away from his table, and I walked toward him with my arms outstretched to greet him before he saw me. When he looked at me, I could see that he did not recognize me, as I apparently did not look like my earth self. In fact, he seemed surprised that someone whom he considered important was coming to greet him. He respectfully rose and received the hug I gave him, a bit hesitantly at first, then he acknowledged my identity and our connection. I attributed his initial lack of recognition to the fact that he was seeing my spirit and not my body.

The bond between parents and children is maintained despite a change in dimension. On earth such a bond creates within the child a need to fulfill parental expectations. I remember observing how Galen experienced this need from the beginning, although what his mother hoped for him and what I hoped for him were not the same.

Days after my dream about encountering my father I was told our meeting was a means of preparing him to remember his earth family so that he could connect with them again from the other side. Thus a primary message of our hug was to spark the recollection of a family agreement.

I think the necessity for awakening such a memory has to do with the notion "out of sight, out of mind." When we are distanced from something for a while, we forget about it and need to encounter it again to remember our experiences with it—just like when we bite into our first peach of the summer and say, "I forgot how good this tastes." In the dream, my father may have already been moving toward choosing to not hold his form in that dimension. As Galen has pointed out, when it comes time for my father to move to another experience he will need to once again assume form, start attending classes again, and regain memory, so that he is not aloof in his next incarnation.

The advantages of choosing to spend time formless in Galen's dimension may not seem clear. Perhaps it fulfills a deep desire of those who are weary from their earth experiences and need a respite from them; after all, nearly everyone enjoys drifting off to sleep under an umbrella on a warm, inviting beach. As for me, a person who gets reenergized by each new change in my life, at a certain point I want to move on to another experience. Ultimately it is impossible to understand such a choice from our third-dimensional perspective.

CHAPTER 16

Angels

Now that I have become better integrated into this dimension, it feels more like home. As a result, I have begun to understand the functioning of the unique beings who are attracted to this dimension because they are committed to the evolution of others, teachers who have given me a great advantage due to the knowledge they have imparted. Even though they have different appearances, personalities, and dialects, they radiate a certain recognizable vibration that draws individuals to them and their teachings. Their energy causes an individual to relate to their lectures on a personal level. Every student in a classroom has the same experience due to the energy of the teacher, which is the same vibration as that of all teachers. Unlike on earth, where an individual feels they have to learn because they are in the presence of a teacher, here I *want* to learn and am willing to open up, understand, and evolve. It is unlikely that anyone sitting in a classroom here doesn't want to learn.

In spite of the many different belief systems people have concerning life in human form or beyond, teachers here are able to connect with them all. So if someone sitting next to me in class has a completely different belief system from mine, we will each hear what the teacher is saying in the context of our own beliefs. For example, if they believe that snow is purple and the sky is orange, they will have no difficulty integrating the day's lecture into that paradigm. Teachers do not try to change anyone's belief system, although they will provide an opportunity for individuals to reevaluate any beliefs that do not lead to balance.

The sole purpose of teachers here is to promote insight and connection within ourselves. These individuals, distinguishable by their vibration, are what on earth would be called angels. Their function does not derive from religion; nor are they considered closer to God. They are simply a lineage of beings with a certain energy who are dedicated to the evolution of those transitioning out of physical bodies: they meet people transitioning into this dimension, then may further assist with the integration as personal teachers.

Because of their unique energy patttterns, teachers hold both authority and mystery. For instance, when I have a question I simply open up with the desire to speak with my personal teacher and there he is. I have seen the teachers of others with questions show up this way as well. They simply walk out of thin air. And they have the same vibration as my teacher, as well as those in classrooms.

Teachers are friendly and caring, making us feel welcome, safe, and loved, yet we never regard them as our best friends because relating with them does not involve emotional intimacy rooted in shared experience. By contrast, because of some shared experiences I developed a very close connection with a being named Brock, although we were from different planets in different dimensions; we shared the agreement to incarnate, which alone had created a bond. I even have a close relationship with Wyrme—as close a relationship as one can have with a fuzzy tube.

Similarly with Arthur and Eileen, the elderly couple who help hold up the energetic fabric of this dimension, I can sense an emotional connection although they themselves have chosen to avoid interaction.

The teachers, while lacking any emotional involvement with us, affect us deeply without ever touching us. They promote insight within us by sparking information we already carry inside us, which brings on epiphany after epiphany, lighting the way to peace. Thus, in imbuing their charges with wisdom they foster in each one of them a sense of connectedness.

The energy of these teaching angels makes up the fabric of the universe, so that even on earth when one has an epiphany there is a good chance it was inspired by such a presence. While still in my earth body, in quiet moments I could feel the pulse of this connectedness and then the epiphany it ignites. Souls that choose to learn through physical incarnations are forever changed by such experiences.

✎ ✎ ✎

Editor's note: An encounter I had with the type of angelic being Galen describes brought me a sense of love and compassion one night when my grief from Galen's passing was still fresh. My bedroom was pitch black and I was in a state between waking and sleeping, and even though my eyes were closed I saw her with my feelings. As she approached from my left, all I could think about was how lovely she was, although I could not make out her face. She bent over me draping her long brown hair over my left side, completing an arc she was making from my right. She had a unique vibration I will never forget, and the love coming from her was overwhelming. Then my body started convulsing in wave after wave of grief. I was in the presence of an angel with whom I desperately wanted to connect and yet all I could do was project up dark emotion. But that was why she was there, to help take grief from me. So I am able to testify that not only can such beings be felt on earth, as Galen states, but that there is a special division of such beings who intercede with those who are grieving because of a deep connection with someone who has passed, comforting them and leaving a strong impression of the vibration of love and compassion from another dimension.

Epilogue

It is common here to have a deep connection to family and friends left behind on earth. Each of us has a longing to know how our families are doing and how a particular choice made here has affected our loved ones on earth. It was my good fortune to have a parent who was open to the communication despite the grief he was experiencing.

In addition to grief, limiting belief systems can make it difficult for people on earth to welcome contact from loved ones on this side. From our perspective, there should be nothing eerie or frightening about such contact, and no fear that those attempting to reach out are "stuck" or hanging around as ghosts. We reach out to ask about the well-being of family members and to let loved ones know that we are fine, free of pain and fear of any kind. Regardless of how we passed, if we are conscious of the experience, as most are, we tend to reach out to loved ones soon after transitioning into this dimension.

Often we communicate through images in dreams or through songs, which is how I first reached my father to let him know I was fine. Yet no matter how we communicate or how resistant those on earth may be to hearing from us, it is of great importance to "listen" to our messages. Doing so will help a person establish a connection with a loved one who has passed, thereby easing the grief, and also help pave the way for their own transition in the future. In a sense, the energy we send to loved ones on earth is like mother's milk, nourishing them in their lives on earth and preparing them for their own journeys afterward.

Communication back to the earth can be difficult, however, especially for parents who have left behind a child they can no longer care for. Many times, teachers remain with such parents to help create a special orb of energy that will offer continual protection until the child becomes mature enough to be self-sufficient. This is the closest a child can come to experiencing an angelic presence without having an actual angel present.

When no one on earth is receptive to our overtures, we are left to process everything in this dimension alone. Such a situation can hamper our progress here. For instance, the fact that my dad has been in constant contact with me since I passed has helped me understand much more about my family, allowing me to quickly progress to the point where I am now assisting others as they come in.

It is important to realize that the quality of communication from this dimension to earth can change over time. People who show up in a dream soon after passing will seem different when they appear again fifteen years later. Some may argue that is just the brain responding differently over the course of time. However, the truth is that individuals here move away from their earth personality as they integrate into this dimension, causing the nature of their contact with loved ones to change.

In fact, after five or six years of contact the potential for clear exchanges may dissipate. The contact can feel less like a departed loved one standing at the other side of a door sending a message and more like they are communicating on a symbolic level. It is not that the deceased in such instances have given up on their families, but rather that they have further integrated into this dimension. To better understand the situation, imagine someone's transition as a new flower bud opening and the bloom lasting five or six years, during which time the communication with loved ones on earth is like rain and sunshine on the petals of the flower. Then the flower closes, containing seeds of new energy, critical information that can prepare those on earth for their own transition and help those on this side with their progress, such as making choices about whether to immediately return to earth or hold a form here as a teacher, helper, or healer.

As difficult as it may be to stay open through intense grief, know that your loved one may be trying to converse with you and do your best to remain receptive to any message coming through. Regard it not as a cause for fear or discomfort, but rather as a gift to you. Even if you receive just one dream—a one-time experience that lets you know everything is okay—the message given and received completes a cycle.

∽ ∽ ∽

Editor's note: Galen has said that belief systems determine the experience we encounter on the other side, that we are confronted not by some outside force, such as religious figures directing humanity's behavior, but by aspects of our inner nature driving our potential benevolence. The implication is that the Jesus, Allah, Buddha, or Moses some meet on the other side are in fact aspects of the individuals meeting them. Those who believe Jesus will walk with them after they pass are likely to have that experience—not with the actual historical teacher but with a benevolent presence they believe is Jesus. Likewise, those who become martyrs believing they will find themselves in heaven with seventy virgins will encounter them; however, they will always remain virgins because that was the strongly held belief.

By contrast, our earth-held belief that whatever exists outside of us is somehow greater than us will dissolve very quickly on the other side, which is actually not a photonic extension of life on earth but rather a destination equipped to take us to a more universal level. Thus while we bring our cherished beliefs there with us, those that are not aligned with the benevolence of the universe will be gently transformed.

Such transformation may require us to look at the suffering we created on earth. For instance, if, in utilizing human experience, we lived as murderers or power-hungry cheaters, then understanding how such an experience served our growth and that of others might be obtained through a role reversal in the next incarnation.

Eventually everything that lingers in the cause-and-effect field forming the basis of physical life on earth will dissolve, and along with it the polarity that informs our current worldview here. In the process, religious dogma will come to be seen as a series of noninteractive illusions that are self-created within various belief structures. Efforts directed toward disseminating hatred and fear will come to be regarded as self-aggrandizing means of asserting one's personal power. With their dissolution comes the realization that we live in a world no longer polarized into "them and us."

Many individuals who instinctively sense higher dimensions believe that something good awaits them after they die. And something good does await them, as well as everyone else, upon realizing that they created their circumstances on earth. Galen indicated that it does not take long for people who have passed to recognize this truth. He explained that individuals who envision walking in the garden with Jesus experience comfort and light in the form of Jesus until they understand that life on earth is heaven or hell depending on people's behaviors; that there is no punishment in the afterlife; and that the desire to love and serve is not imposed upon us but emanates from our true nature. He also said that martyrs eventually recognize images of the seventy virgins as representative of new ideas and beginnings they shunned while on earth—a discovery that comes on the heels of understanding that they always had the opportunity to change and that nothing, including their own souls, forced them to make the choices they did. Whether or not people "behave" themselves matters a great deal, he explained, for this is a benevolent universe in which compassion and love are rewarded and allow one to evolve on both a personal and soul level.

Because this is a benevolent universe, everything eventually is brought back to a state of harmony. For one thing, this means that misusing our power requires us to regain balance, which apparently can take many lifetimes. For those with a diabolic plan to destroy life, there is a dimension in which these inclinations can be worked out, I have been told, but it is not a realm most people would want to spend time in, let alone visit. For individuals whose tendency toward malevolence is so severe that their soul determines there can be no redemption, it withdraws the life force from that personality, which will then be left to dissipate as if it were a diseased limb of a tree cut off to decompose in a compost pile. But for the vast majority of humanity, our destiny within a benevolent universe is to come into balance in the present or subsequent lifetime by recognizing that we are responsible for the life we live on earth, as well as for the lives of others. When we foster love and harmony during our sojourns on earth, we create compassion, connection, and a place for ourselves and others in a unified field.

So it is that in passing out of our earth bodies we are given an opportunity to assess how our beliefs and behaviors served the best interests of all. None of us gets a free pass to do as we wish. Seen from the perspective of the other side, every life chapter counts and every one of us matters.

Acknowledgments

My gratitude to Audrey Wrinkles (bluespiralhand@yahoo.com), a trance medium I first investigated in 1996, who was present for me the night of Galen's crossing. The guides she and I work with, a collective consciousness that identify themselves as Rietta Tau Bien, trained me for two years before Galen asked me to be a scribe for his experience on the other side. Without the continued assistance of Audrey and Rietta, the Death Walker series could not have been written.

About the Author

Galen Stoller was in many respects an all-American kid. He liked going to theme parks and movies, visiting his grandparents, hamming it up at school, and hanging out with his friends. Steeped in the world of sci-fi/fantasy, he read the complete Harry Potter series, the Golden Compass/Dark Material series, and the Bartimaeus Trilogy. He also read the C.S. Lewis Narnia series over and over, except for the last book, in which all the protagonists were killed in a train accident—a volume he read once and never wanted to return to.

It was a train accident that would take Galen's earth life when he was sixteen years old. At the time, Galen was in eleventh grade at Desert Academy in Santa Fe, New Mexico, and starting to think about enrolling in college. An accomplished actor, he was about to perform the dual roles of Fagan and Bill Sikes in *Oliver!* He was an ethical vegetarian and helped train dogs for Assistance Dogs of the West. Because of this service, he was nominated posthumously for the 2008 Amy Biel Youth Spirit Award. Following the second anniversary of his passing, he asked his father to start writing *My Life after Life*, the first book in what he called the Death Walker series.

About the Editor

K Paul Stoller, MD, started his medical career as a pediatrician and was a Diplomat of the American Board of Pediatrics for over two decades. Previously, in the early 1970s, he was a University of California President's Undergraduate Fellow in the Health Sciences, working in the UCLA Department of Anesthesiology and volunteering at the since disbanded Parapsychology Lab at the UCLA Neuropsychiatric Institute. He matriculated at Penn State and then completed his postgraduate training at UCLA.

His first published works, papers on psychopharmacology, came to print before he entered medical school. During medical school, he was hired to do research for the Humane Society of the United States and became involved in an effort to prohibit the use of shelter dogs for medical experiments, which made him very unpopular in certain circles when he published an article entitled "Sewer Science and Pound Seizure" in the *International Journal for the Study of Animal Problems*. He was then invited to become a founding board member of the Humane Farming Association, and served as science editor for the *Animal's Voice Magazine*, where he was nominated for a Maggie Award.

In the mid-1990s, after a friend, the head of Apple Computer's Advanced Technology Group, lapsed into a coma, Dr. Stoller began investigating hyperbaric medicine. Soon after, he started administering hyperbaric oxygen to brain-injured children and adults, including Iraqi vets and retired NFL players with traumatic brain injuries, also pioneering the use of this therapy for treating children with fetal alcohol syndrome. He is a Fellow of the American College of Hyperbaric Medicine and has served as president of the International Hyperbaric Medical Association for almost a decade.

When his son was killed in a train accident in 2007, he discovered the effectiveness of the hormone oxytocin in treating pathological grief. Dr. Stoller, who has medical offices in Santa Fe, Sacramento, and San Francisco, is also the editor of *My Life after Life: A Posthumous Memoir* and the author of *Oxytocin: The Hormone of Healing and Hope*.